D1458319

Sport in the Market?

*The Economic Causes and Consequences
of the 'Packer Revolution'*

PETER J. SLOANE

*Professor of Economics and Management,
Paisley College of Technology*

Published by

THE INSTITUTE OF ECONOMIC AFFAIRS

1980

First published in April 1980

© THE INSTITUTE OF ECONOMIC AFFAIRS 1980

ISSN 0073-2818
ISBN 0-255 36130-0

Printed in England by

GORON PRO-PRINT CO LTD
6 Marlborough Road, Churchill Industrial Estate, Lancing, Sussex

Text set in 'Monotype' Baskerville

CONTENTS

[5]

PREFACE

The *Hobart Papers* are intended to contribute a stream of authoritative, independent and lucid analyses to the understanding and application of economics to private and government activity. The characteristic theme has been the optimum use of scarce resources and the extent to which it can best be achieved in markets within an appropriate framework or, where markets cannot work, in other ways. Since the alternative to the market is, in practice, the state, and both are imperfect, the choice between them should effectively depend on judgement of the comparative consequence of 'market failure' and 'government failure'.

Throughout its life the Institute has sought to apply market analysis to subjects that are not normally thought to be the province of the economist. Hobart Paper 85 by Professor Peter J. Sloane represents an effort to examine recent trends in sport in Britain (and other countries) to see how far economics can shed light on its development when it is analysed as selling a service for which spectators will pay, and therefore with components of supply and demand that determine the price at which it can be produced.

Professor Sloane opens with a discussion of the nature of the service that sport supplies in order to attract its market of spectators or 'fans'. He argues that sports teams have to provide an uncertain outcome so that the spectators are not witnessing a pre-determined contest. The importance of this view is that it seems to provide a reason for restricting competition in league clubs. At one point he divides spectators into two parts, the partisans who want their team to win and the connoisseurs of the sport who come to watch good play. The connoisseurs want the excitement of seeing which side wins; but the partisans want the satisfaction of seeing their side win whatever its merits. The product therefore differs for the two kinds of consumer. In some events partisans may outnumber connoisseurs; the case for restricting competition thus seems to turn on whether the connoisseurs outnumber the partisans. It remains true that teams provide a joint product, and that,

[7]

although teams compete for players, they do not compete with one another as do firms making distinct products.

After discussing sport in macro-economic terms—its total national size and the extent to which the demand for it as a whole varies with income and other conditions—Professor Sloane moves to the central part of his analysis, the micro-economic supply of sport and the demand for it. Here he analyses the economics of the individual team and the leagues into which teams are grouped to provide the spectacle of individual skill and team co-operation. He reviews developments in baseball and other American sports and then arrives at the subject that will be most in the minds of British readers: the broad comparison between soccer and cricket, the former more competitive until recent years than the latter, and the increase in competition in organising cricket accompanying the Packer development.

Feelings in Britain ran high when the Packer 'invasion' was first announced. Whatever the cultural or other elements in cricket, or in sport generally, the economic aspects of supply, demand and price cannot be excluded or ignored. The people who enjoy watching cricket as a game, or who regard it as embodying the national spirit in some sense, must take into account the costs involved in alternative policies: methods of organising sport, the rules governing competition for players or the working of leagues, the sources of income from gate revenue, advertising, sponsors, and other policies. Even if we preferred that cricket or other sports should not be subject to commercial pressures, it is relevant to know what the economic pros and cons are before attitudes can be formed rationally. The interesting question here is why the conduct of cricket produced a Packer, and whether a Kerry Packer or anyone else would have appeared sooner or later. The issues are basically economic rather than personal.

Professor Sloane's analysis is thus of interest not only to students and teachers of economics but also to people who enjoy cricket and other sports.

The Institute has to thank Professors S. C. Littlechild and Basil S. Yamey for reading all or part of an early draft and offering comments that Professor Sloane has borne in mind in his final revisions. By its constitution the Institute must dissociate its Trustees, Directors and Advisory Council from the analysis of its authors but offers this *Hobart Paper* as a rare economic analysis of a subject that is of wide interest to the British public and an industry with economic aspects that require to be understood if it is to develop with satisfaction to players as well as to spectators.

February 1980   ARTHUR SELDON

THE AUTHOR

PETER J. SLOANE is Professor of Economics and Management at Paisley College of Technology, Scotland. He was born in 1942 and educated at the Universities of Sheffield and Strathclyde. From 1966 to 1975 he held lecturing posts at the Universities of Aberdeen and Nottingham. In 1973-74 he was seconded to the Department of Employment's Unit for Manpower Studies as Economic Adviser, and in 1978 was Visiting Professor in the Faculty of Business, McMaster University, Canada. He has acted as consultant to the National Board for Prices and Incomes, the Office of Manpower Economics, the Commission on Industrial Relations, the Royal Commission on the Distribution of Income and Wealth, the Social Science Research Council, the International Labour Office, the Organisation for Economic Co-operation and Development and the Commission of the European Communities. He is a member of the Economics Board of the Council for National Academic Awards, and of the Economics Committee of the Social Science Research Council, where he is also a member of Council.

Professor Sloane has written studies on the economics of sport in the *British Journal of Industrial Relations,* the *Scottish Journal of Political Economy,* the *Journal of Industrial Relations* (Australia), and the *Bulletin of Economic Research.* In 1971 he was a member of a Conference of Experts on the Economics of Sport, at The Brookings Institution, Washington DC, and in 1978 a participant in the First World Congress of Sports Sciences, Cordoba, Argentina. He has also written widely as author or editor on labour economics and industrial relations.

ACKNOWLEDGEMENTS

I am grateful to Arthur Seldon and Dr Alistair Young for many helpful comments on an early draft of this *Paper.* David Strachan of the Paisley College Library was particularly helpful in obtaining obscure references to recent developments in professional sports. Mr E. Walker, Secretary of the Scottish Football Association, kindly provided me with a copy of the new Union of European Football Associations' rules on the transfer of players within the EEC. Jean Beggs, my secretary, managed as always to make sense out of nonsense in typing the manuscript.

January 1980   P. J. S.

GLOSSARY

CROSS-SECTION DATA—Statistical series of recordings of economic information for a number of individuals (or firms or countries or other units) at the same moment or period of time.

DIMINISHING RETURNS—The eventual tendency for output to increase at a diminishing rate with an increase in the input of a factor of production, other inputs being held constant.

DUOPOLY—A market in which there are only two *sellers* of the product, for example, two sports leagues in competition with each other for spectators.

DUOPSONY—A market in which there are only two *buyers* of the factors of production, for example, two sports leagues in competition with each other for players.

EXPLOITATION—The payment to labour of a wage lower than its worth as measured by its marginal revenue product (below). This is likely to occur in monopsonistic markets (below) which are typical of professional team sports. Exploitation should not be confused with payment of low wages—it is concerned solely with payment relative to productivity.

INFERIOR GOOD—A product bought in relatively large quantities out of a small income and for which demand falls as income rises.

MARGINAL REVENUE PRODUCT (MRP)/MARGINAL PRODUCTIVITY OF LABOUR—The increment in the total value of output obtained from the employment of an extra worker. In professional team sports it is not possible to increase the number of players in a team, since this is proscribed by the rules. Hence marginal revenue product should be thought of in relation to increases in player quality (or the incremental value added to the team's output by a newly-bought star player).

MAXIMAND—The variable (e.g. quantity) which is sought to be maximised—for a firm its profits or sales.

MICRO-ECONOMICS—The analysis of the allocation of resources at a disaggregated level such as within an enterprise (firm, etc.) or a market.

MONOPSONY—A market in which there is only one buyer for the factors of production (e.g. a club which holds the contract of a player who is not free to move to other clubs).

PRICE ELASTICITY OF DEMAND—The responsiveness of quantity demanded to changes in price. Demand is said to be elastic when a change in price leads to a more than proportionate change in quantity demanded, and inelastic when such a change leads to a less than proportionate change in quantity. Similarly, INCOME-ELASTICITY is the responsiveness of demand to changes in income.

PRODUCTION FUNCTION—The relationship between inputs of factors of production and outputs of goods (in the context of professional team sports between the performance of individual players and team success).

REVENUE FUNCTION—The relationship between productivity and revenue (in the context of professional team sports between team success and income from gate receipts and other sources of revenue).

WORKABLE COMPETITION—A market structure in which there are relatively few firms but where efficiency is maintained through innovation based on the threat of new entry.

I. INTRODUCTION

It is not difficult to justify an examination of the economics of sport. Sporting activities of various types are an important part of the everyday life of a large number of citizens in virtually all countries and clearly have economic implications. Whilst the total or national 'macro-economic' importance of sport in the gross domestic product is relatively small (p. [7]), it possesses some attributes of a quasi-public good because it is said to yield 'external benefits' in the form of a healthy population and prestige to countries successful in international competition. (A 'public good' is normally defined as one that cannot be physically or economically refused to 'free riders' who refuse to pay, such as a playing field prohibitively expensive to fence in and police.) It is presumably for these external benefits that governments have created Ministers of Sport and that many sporting facilities are provided by government rather than private enterprise, though in essence sport is not a public good because there is no difficulty in excluding would-be consumers who do not pay. (Sports centres, although often provided by local government and subsidised from rates and taxes, are also *not* a public good in this sense.)

(a) *Issues in professional team sports*

Professional team sports became established in the latter part of the 19th century and have frequently occasioned controversy about such issues as professionalism *versus* amateurism, the behaviour of club organisers, managers, players and spectators, and the limitation on players' freedom to move between employing clubs. With the growth of the professional sports business not only on a national but also on an international basis, some issues appear to have become even more prominent in recent years. Challenges to the established sports have occurred in several sports. In lawn tennis the professional World Tennis (WCT) organisation was formed as a competitor (for spectators) with the established amateur game and the temporary boycott of Wimbledon by some professional

[13]

players. In cricket Kerry Packer's short-lived World Series Cricket (WSC) created competition to the established authorities. And in soccer professional soccer leagues in North America have employed players from various parts of the world. Particularly in soccer, players fought successfully for (partial) freedom of contract at the same time as transfer fees reached new heights—in excess of £1 million in the transfer of Trevor Francis from Birmingham City to Nottingham Forest and more recently almost £1·5 million in the transfers of Steve Daley to Manchester City and Andy Gray to Wolverhampton Wanderers.

Despite widespread interest in the major sports (and the willingness to spend large sums of money on players in some), many soccer and cricket clubs in Britain have suffered from severe financial problems and the threat of closure. Questions have been raised about the efficiency of both league and club managements. Would many of these financial problems disappear if leagues operated with fewer clubs or revised their price and marketing policies? Does a black market in tickets for major games such as the FA Cup Final indicate that prices have been set too low for profit maximisation?

It is hoped this *Hobart Paper* will provide a framework for understanding and analysing these issues in order to predict developments and suggest policies for improving the conduct and performance of the sports industry by action both from the governing bodies of the sports themselves and from government.

(b) The peculiarities of professional team sports

This *Paper* focusses on the *micro-economics** of the supply by 'firms' (clubs) of professional sporting contests in a market in which consumers are spectators rather than participants. It concentrates on professional team sports rather than on contests among individuals like boxing, wrestling, billiards and snooker. Team sports include football (of various varieties), rugby league, cricket, speedway, basketball, baseball and ice-hockey. Sports such as athletics, cycling, golf, tennis, show-jumping and motor sports include some elements of both individual and team sports, but here team tournaments have not been as important commercially as competition amongst

*Glossary.

[14]

individuals. In tennis the development of the team sport has been a very recent phenomenon.[1] This suggests that the distinction may sometimes be based on tradition rather than on the inherent nature of the sport. The emphasis is on team sports both because they generally possess the most highly developed economic aspects and because the necessity of maintaining sporting equality among teams in order to maintain consumer-spectator interest has led to restrictions of competition which would be unacceptable in other industries.

A definition of team sports

A professional team sport is a contest for which spectators pay an admission charge and in which an equal number of participants (or individual players) are divided into two competing teams to form a game. A number of teams form a league and each team competes against every other team in the league over a specified period or season. In an individual sport, on the other hand, individual contestants compete against one another in a tournament, or each contestant faces another sequentially on a knock-out basis, the winner at each stage going on to successive rounds until only one—the champion— is left. A closely-fought tournament between *individuals* of roughly equal ability may, as in boxing, also attract a larger number of spectators than one in which the outcome is a foregone conclusion. But here playing resources cannot be redistributed to maximise uncertainty of outcome. Some form of handicapping, as in golf or horse-racing, may then be introduced to maintain the competitive equality of opportunity to win.

The nature of the product

The central theme of this *Paper,* accepted to varying degrees by most economists who have analysed the subject, is that the economics of team sports are peculiar because it is not possible to provide its product, entertainment, without the assistance of other teams (rival producers). In competitive industry, competition drives out the inefficient producer so that only efficient and viable firms remain. In professional team sports,

---

[1] Though here spectator interest has been muted, perhaps by the failure to associate players clearly with particular geographical areas.

in contrast, individual clubs (producers) have a vested interest not only in the continued existence of other clubs, but also in their economic viability as competitors in order to maximise the interest of spectators and hence revenues from the sale of the product (the joint game). The nature of the product thus creates the requirement for uncertainty of outcome.

This approach has led in turn to queries among economists whether the league rather than the club is the equivalent of the 'firm' in the normal competitive industry analysed by economic theory, or whether the league is more appropriately analysed as a cartel which, amongst other things, cross-subsidises its members. This is the approach adopted here. Questions are also raised about the objectives of the people who control the clubs. Those who regard sporting activity as a pastime for patrons or sponsors rather than a business might argue that profit maximisation, for example, has little to do with the observed behaviour of sporting authorities. Rich businessmen, it seems, are often prepared, perhaps for motives of prestige, to invest considerable sums of money in the clubs they control without the prospect of a market rate of return. Association with a club could thus be regarded as a form of consumption rather than production. In the sports sector, also, external sources of income from sponsorship by industry, television and elsewhere are much more significant than in most industries.

It is perhaps in the market for sports 'labour' that the most distinctive features are found.[1] Since the number of players in a team is fixed, labour quality becomes of paramount importance. For this and other reasons, such as the desire to preserve uncertainty of outcome, restrictive rules have been devised to create property rights over the players for individual clubs.

We must also consider the possibility that the market is inherently unstable. Since it is not feasible for all teams to be successful (in the sporting sense) at any one time, revenues will be lower for the unsuccessful. The question is then whether the sports industry should be exempted from the requirements of monopoly and restrictive practices legislation.

---

[1] The product market and labour market are inter-related even more closely than in the conventional industrial case since spectators actually pay to observe the 'productive process'.

(c) Issues to be considered

We analyse first of all the nature of the market for the product (II). The demand for sport in general is examined to establish whether lack of competition in the industry may have led to a failure to exploit to the full the potential of the market. Then we examine in some detail the elements determining the demand for professional sporting competitions to ascertain whether it is likely that some clubs will tend to dominate, thereby reducing uncertainty of outcome. The motivation of club owners and controllers (relevant to the question whether the market will itself rectify serious imbalances in sporting competition) and the behaviour of sporting leagues as cartels are also examined here.

III discusses forms of restriction on mobility in the labour market (controls on entry, transfer between clubs, and payment) and examines the possibility of exploitation of labour by the clubs.

IV focusses on recent developments, including both increased freedom in the player market and increased competition through the entry of entrepreneurs into the product market. It considers whether a competitive factor market is viable in professional sports and whether sports leagues are natural monopolies.

In the concluding sections (V and VI) the effects of new competition are analysed and policy proposals made. Here the organisation of professional team sports may be viewed from several perspectives.

First, club owners are concerned that their clubs should remain as viable entities (long-run survival) or that they should provide an adequate return on the investment in sporting activities (including due allowance for non-pecuniary benefits).

Second, players are concerned with the amount of their remuneration and other terms of employment.

Third, and above all, spectators (consumers) have an interest in the quality of the product they pay for.

These interests may sometimes conflict. Higher profitability may imply fewer clubs, which has the consequence of reduced employment prospects for players and fewer towns with

[17]

membership of the league. In normal circumstances we would expect the outcome to be determined by the market. We will find that, although there are special circumstances in sport, 'market forces' are at work, especially in the long run.

II. THE PRODUCT MARKET

(a) The demand for sport

As real incomes rise and hours of work diminish we would expect that the demand for leisure goods, including professional sports, would rise. There has been a dramatic growth of outdoor activities which involve participation rather than spectating. Participants in camping rose from 25,000 in 1950 to 385,000 in 1977, in walking and climbing from 219,000 to 350,000, in water sports from 1,000 to 84,000; the number of fishing licences issued rose from 387,000 to 1,231,000; and membership of the English Golf Union rose from 131,000 to 450,000.[1]

Post-war decline in professional team sports in the UK

Yet the demand for the product of British professional team sports has in general fallen from its peak after the Second World War. Unless such sports are what economists call 'inferior goods', the consumption of which falls absolutely as incomes rise, it would seem, therefore, that the organisers have not made the most of their market opportunities. It is true that the range of competing leisure goods has widened, in particular television.[2] But the experience of North American professional team sports, which display general profitability and growth, suggests that a change in tastes cannot be the whole explanation for the fall in demand for the products of British professional team sports.

On this view, the development of prospering American professional soccer leagues and the influx of foreign players, coaches and managers, including many from Britain, may in the long run present a stronger challenge to professional soccer

---

[1] Central Statistical Office, *Social Trends*, HMSO (annually). An exception to this growth was cycling, where numbers fell from 121,000 in 1950 to 43,000 in 1977.

[2] The competitive effects of television ownership on other forms of entertainment are most clearly seen in the cinema. Cinema attendance figures have declined dramatically since the mid-1950s when television ownership began to expand. In 1953 the average weekly cinema audience was some 25 million; in 1975 below 2½ million. That such trends are not immutable if attention is paid to the product is indicated by the 20 per cent rise in cinema attendances in 1978.

than did, temporarily, the Packer competition to professional cricket. Although the competition from WSC occurred in the same geographical markets as the established game, there remained the possibility of a return to product market monopoly in cricket (Section V). In soccer there is a major new market to be developed in competition with other sports in the larger North American cities. With the skilled marketing expertise common in North America, it is likely under present circumstances to continue to drain away the best talent from other countries for many years, with a consequent decline in quality. This increased international market for players, already widened through the free labour market of the EEC, may force the established national leagues of Europe to develop their market potential more fully.

Inadequate official statistics

Published official data are inadequate to enable clear predictions to be made of the likely demand for professional sports. Consumer expenditure (at current prices) on miscellaneous leisure goods rose from £404 million in 1963 (or 2·0 per cent of national total consumer expenditure) to £1,032 million (or 2·3 per cent) in 1973.[1] Similarly, expenditure on entertainment and recreational services rose from £344 million (1·7 per cent) in 1963 to £842 million (1·9 per cent) in 1973. Gambling on sporting outcomes is also an important item of expenditure, since it may serve to increase interest in the sports themselves (and hence attendances), as well as providing them with income from fixture list copyright or pools run by the clubs themselves. It is estimated that over one-third of adults enter football pool competitions; in 1977 they staked £233 million. These limited statistics suggest that consumers are able and prepared to spend a larger proportion of their income on sport and related leisure pursuits if supplied to satisfy their wishes, preferences and circumstances.

Main factors in leisure participation

Six main factors determine participation in leisure facilities: age, sex, social class, income, car ownership and education,[2] though they will influence the sports in diverse ways. The most

---

[1] *National Income and Expenditure 1963-73*, HMSO, is the source of these data.

[2] According to the 1973 *General Household Survey* (GHS). The GHS is a continuous survey of individual households.

TABLE I

SPECTATORS OF SELECTED SPORTS: BY SEX, GREAT BRITAIN, 1973 AND 1977

Spectators as a Percentage of All Adults
(in the four weeks before interview)

Sport watched	1973		1977	
	Men %	Women %	Men %	Women %
Soccer	10·3	1·4	7·4	1·2
Rugby	n.a.	n.a.	1·3	0·3
Cricket	1·2	0·5	1·0	0·4
Motor sports	1·1	0·5	1·2	0·5
Horse-racing	0·6	0·4	0·8	0·5

Source: General Household Surveys, 1973 and 1977.

popular sports amongst people in professional occupations are tennis, golf, squash, badminton and fives; the most popular among manual workers are darts, billiards and snooker.[1] For some socio-economic groups, taking part in sport may compete with watching it; but since participation in most sports declines with age, earlier participation in youth may be related to spectating in older age-groups.[2] In 1977 6 per cent of adult males participated in soccer, 4 per cent in golf, 2 per cent in cricket and 1 per cent in rugby, but the figure for soccer in the 16-24 age-group was no less than 20 per cent.

Soccer is also the most popular spectator sport, though recording a lower percentage figure in 1977 than in 1973 (Table I). The considerable difference between the percentage of men and of women watching sports suggests that all sports may have considerable potential for expanding the number of spectators by marketing the product as family entertainment, especially, though not only, in soccer.[3] 16 per cent of

[1] The GHS gives information on the socio-economic group patterns of sporting activities.

[2] Over 40 per cent of all spectators at soccer games are in the 25-44 age-group; the 16-24 age-group provides nearly a quarter of all spectators.

[3] This could in part reflect differences between men and women, at least working women, in the time they devote to leisure activity. A survey of work and leisure hours in the London metropolitan region in 1970, reported in *Social Trends*, found that married men aged 30-49 spent 31·7 hours per week in leisure activities and wives in this age-group, working full-time, 25·7 hours (women working part-time 31·2 hours, women not in paid work 44·4 hours). Despite the growth

[Continued on page 22]

adult males and 5 per cent of adult females watched one or more sports and games in 1973,[1] but the propensity to spectate declines with age from 22 per cent of males and 10 per cent of females in the 16-19 age-group to 8 per cent of males and 1 per cent of females in the 70 and over age-group. It increases with family income—in 1973, from 4 per cent of all adults with family incomes of £25 a week and below to 15 per cent of all adults with family incomes above £80 a week, compared with an average of 11 per cent. Car ownership is also significant: 12 per cent of the car-owning population watch sports and games compared to 8 per cent without cars. 14 per cent of skilled manual workers and 7 per cent of unskilled manual workers are spectators; the non-manual groups fall into the upper part of the range.[2] Data for the length of education reveal that 8 per cent of people who left school at 14 are spectators, compared with 13 per cent who left at ages 15, 16 and 18, and 14 per cent who left at 17.[3] Finally, there are some significant regional differences. Only 8 per cent of the adult population are spectators in Yorkshire and Humberside compared with 13 per cent in Scotland.

In general these statistics cast doubt on the view that sports spectating is an *inferior good.** The *cross-section data** suggest that demand rises with income, car ownership, skill and education, though we cannot identify the independent effect of each. The data are not published separately for individual sports, but it is clear that a detailed knowledge of the composi-

[*Continued from page 21*]

of leisure time with reduced hours of work some sports, notably cricket, are of course very time-consuming. The move to one-day cricket in contrast to three-day championship games may reflect the increased competition for scarce leisure time as the value of time spent on other activities rises with income, which puts new leisure activities like sailing within the reach of more people.

[1] The GHS statistics include watching as a spectator (except on TV) soccer, rugby, cricket and other team sports (bowls, hockey, tennis, etc.); horse riding, show jumping, riding/equestrian events; motor/motor cycle sports, stock-car racing; water sports (e.g. swimming, water-skiing and sailing, etc.); other outdoor activities (e.g. cycle races, athletics, hound trails, greyhounds, golf); indoor sports and games (e.g. skating, boxing, wrestling, basketball, ice-hockey).

[2] There may, however, be marked differences between sports. Thus, soccer and rugby league have generally been regarded as 'working class' spectator sports, cricket and rugby union as 'middle class'. Soccer attracts all socio-economic groups: 5 per cent professional, 11 per cent employers and managers, 22 per cent intermediate and junior non-manual (1977 GHS).

[3] These figures may be dominated by age effects, school-leavers at 14 or below falling into the older age categories.

tion of demand for the product would enable each sport to market its product more effectively. It is doubtful whether the various sports have yet attempted to do this seriously, which strongly suggests that there is a lack of competition and of effort to maximise profits (or minimise losses).

(b) The product and competition in professional team sports

What is the product that sports clubs combine together to produce? In economic terms it is not sufficient to sum up the total number of games produced, since we require information on the price that consumers are prepared to pay in order to place a valuation upon them. Thus, as Professor Simon Rottenberg has noted in the first comprehensive economic analysis of professional sports:[1]

> 'Two teams opposed to each other in play are like two firms producing a single product. The product is the game, weighted by the revenues derived from its play. With game admission prices given, the product is the game, weighted by the number of paying customers who attend. When 30,000 attend, the output is twice as large as when 15,000 attend. In one sense, the teams compete; in another, they combine in a single firm in which the success of each branch requires that it be not "too much" more efficient than the other. If it is, output falls.'[2]

This definition implies that an increase in the number of clubs and, therefore, in the context of a league, in the number of games played may not raise total output. If the demand rises as the price falls (i.e. there is a downward sloping demand curve for the product), the larger number of games could be sold only at a lower price. And if the demand rises proportionately less than the fall in price (demand is relatively inelastic), total revenue will fall. Unlike many products, however, consumption is spread over a long period at discrete intervals (the sports season is spread over several months). This may mean that a number of additional games could be sold at existing prices before attendance per game falls off appreciably. Consumption takes place, furthermore, at a limited number of venues (stadia) which are geographically dispersed. The market is therefore segmented, since the majority of spectators will

[1] S. Rottenberg, 'The Baseball Player's Labour Market', *Journal of Political Economy*, June 1956.

[2] Hence there must be 'uncertainty of outcome'.

attend only at one venue, governed by where they live. Except in cities with several clubs, each club is a local monopoly: there are no competing producers in its geographical market area. And even in large cities such as London, geographical separation may result in an effective local monopoly.

TV has the advantage of enabling spectators to watch games regardless of where they live. But at present payment is not directly related to demand as measured by viewing time, though this link could be achieved by Pay-TV.[1]

Importance of quality of product?

More important than price to some or many consumers may be the quality of the product. Whilst each team cannot increase output by increasing the number of players, the quality of their skills may vary considerably. A larger number of spectators will be attracted to the games of a team with several star players than to those of teams containing none. Clubs in various sports are therefore prepared to pay larger transfer fees to obtain the services of star players. This is most clearly seen in soccer, where transfer fees have escalated despite the poor financial circumstances of many clubs. Apart from the transfer fees paid for players such as Francis, Daley and Gray, a number of players have been transferred for fees of over £500,000. This represents a major part of total receipts for one season for even the larger clubs (as well as pre-empting rival clubs from signing the few available star players), and is most easily explained in terms of maximising playing success, further discussed in Sections III and IV. (Another incentive for profitable clubs to sign players for large fees is that it enables them to avoid corporation tax, which suggests they are not profit maximisers concerned with distributing high dividends to shareholders.)

An alternative method might be for clubs to spend more money on improving the skills of existing players. If skill is innate, this would not be practicable. Scarcity of star players will then tend only to force up their price. An improvement in quality should result in a higher standard of performance or more entertaining play: a larger number of goals scored per game by attacking players in soccer, more runs per over by

---

[1] Cf. Sir Sydney Caine, *Paying for TV?*, Hobart Paper 43, IEA, 1968 (and Supplement, *Statement on TV Policy*, IEA, 1969).

batsmen in cricket. An increase in the quality of defensive players in soccer and bowlers in cricket will have the reverse effects. The outcome should be a higher proportion of games won.

Rottenberg suggests that an unchecked improvement in quality, if unequally distributed, will not be an unmixed blessing. What economists call the 'uncertainty of outcome' hypothesis suggests that demand for the product rises the more equally balanced competing teams are. Demand falls the wider is the dispersion of percentages of games won by all teams in the league. In other words, a championship winning team will attract larger attendances, and so too will its rivals, if it wins 55 per cent of its games rather than 85 per cent, because uncertainty about the eventual winner is then maintained for a larger proportion of games in a season. In the short run, perfect equality among teams would seem to imply that every team should win and lose the same number of games over the season. In the long run, equality would imply that the number of league championship wins is shared equally amongst all clubs. Either of these forms of perfect equality would, assuming that each club has equal drawing power, maximise attendances for a given degree of quality.

'Uncertainty of outcome' the key

The uncertainty of outcome in the result of games is the key to the economic analysis of professional team sports. On it rests the justification for sporting leagues restricting competition in the price and output of individual member clubs and in their property rights in players. This is a major explanation for the rules devised to ensure the survival of a sufficient (or desired) number of clubs, through (partial) pooling of revenues and limitations on the mobility of players among clubs. These rules are supplemented by strict controls on entry to protect the local monopolies of existing member clubs. In larger cities with several clubs direct competition is constrained by avoiding fixture clashes as far as possible—a form of market-sharing. An American economist, Professor R. G. Noll, comments on American sport:

'Nearly every phase of a team or league is influenced by practices and rules that limit economic competition within the industry. In most cases government has either sanctioned or failed to attack effectively these anti-competitive practices. Consequently, professional team sports provide economists with a unique opportunity to study the operation and performance of an effective and well-organised cartel'.[1]

But the limitation of competition within a league does not in itself imply that competitive forces are wholly inoperative. Professional team sports must compete with other leisure pursuits for the scarce time and financial resources of consumers. There is also the possibility that rival leagues in the same sport may be formed where monopoly profits are earned or where, through inertia, market potential is not fully exploited. Indeed, Kerry Packer's WSC can be seen as a response to inertia and unexploited potential. Professional team sports organisers, at least in Britain, have not been noteworthy for their rate of product innovation. Outdated stadia, inadequate measures to deal with the effects of inclement weather, poor promotion of the product, failure to extract the maximum income from television authorities, pools promoters and industrial sponsors are all indicative of managements sheltered from the full rigours of competitive forces. The WSC organisers have, in contrast, used modern promotional methods to sell the product and introduced product innovation in the form of floodlit night games (as in soccer) and more professional presentation on North America lines, with significant adverse effects on the revenues of the established cricket authorities.

(c) Measuring the demand for sporting competitions

The suggestion that uncertainty of outcome may require restrictive rules in professional team sports requires that we test whether in practice attendances are adversely affected by inequalities in playing performance. To do this it is necessary to consider all relevant factors determining attendance.

The first is population, since the drawing power of a club varies with the number of persons within travelling distance of the stadium. This determinant of attendance has been found to be important.[2] American analyses can yield crude estimates of the minimum size of population in an area that can sustain

---

[1] *Major League Team Sports*, Social Science Working Paper, No. 125, California Institute of Technology, May 1976.

[2] Numerous American studies provide the evidence for this statement. Unfortunately similar data for British professional team sports are not available.

a major league team in the various sports: the minimum size to ensure profitability for a single club is 900,000 for ice-hockey, 1 million for football (US rules), 1·9 million for baseball and 4 million for basketball.

It does not follow that there is necessarily a constant relation-ship between size of population and attendance. English Football League clubs, for instance, appear to do well if they attract 10 per cent of the local population (crudely defined as resident within the city). But the figure appears to range from less than 2 per cent to more than 20 per cent, leaving aside towns with more than one league team. Ipswich Town in the First Division attracted 20 per cent of the local population in the 1977-78 season, whilst several clubs with more successful playing performance could only attract between 5 and 7 per cent.[1] The opening of a new motorway in Lancashire in 1973 coincided with a significant change in the pattern of attendances at soccer matches among the 10 Lancashire Football League clubs. The proportion of supporters watching matches involving the two Manchester and two Liverpool clubs rose from 50 per cent of attendances in Lancashire in 1961 to 66 per cent in 1971, though there was a decline in total attendances in the county.

Large cities with several clubs might be expected to have lower average attendances, although fixture clashes are generally avoided as far as possible by arranging the home games of neighbouring clubs on different dates, and local rivalry may stimulate demand. Professor P. Rivett,[2] for instance, finds that whilst there appears to be no relationship between the attendances of the two Manchester or two Liverpool clubs, attendances in neighbouring Preston and Blackburn are closely related season by season, regardless of relative success or the division in which each competed. Differences in population size clearly pose a problem for professional team sports, since the clubs with the stronger drawing power will receive larger revenues and the ability to monopolise the services of star players, with consequent inequality of playing performance among member clubs.

[1] In order to isolate the effect of population size it is necessary, however, to hold constant all other relevant factors determining attendance, including in particular playing success. Nonetheless, differences in attendance between cities are so marked as to suggest consumer tastes can vary considerably from one location to another.

[2] 'The Structure of League Football', *Operational Research Quarterly*, Vol. 26, No. 4, 1975.

Implications for sports leagues of population (spectator) potential

The clear implications for the organisation of a league seem to have been appreciated less by sports organisers in the UK than in North America. As far as possible, very large differences in population and hence spectator potential for member clubs should be avoided on the formation of a new league or on contraction or expansion of an existing league. Further, where some cities are very much larger than others, additional league clubs should be formed to minimise differences in spectator potential, regard being paid to differences in spectator enthusiasm or demand for the sport between areas. In the absence of restrictions on entry we would expect the market mechanism to fulfil this function. Where leagues are based on precise geographical divisions, such as the County Cricket Championship or international competitions, it is obviously more difficult to deal with inequalities in population; but the problem is eased by rules specifying in general that players may play only for the county or country of birth. This aspect is discussed more fully in Section III, but could be one source of 'backwardness' in cricket compared with soccer since the incentive to become more efficient in order to attract the better players is reduced.

Clubs are indivisible entities. A particular location may be larger (in population) than the minimum size necessary to support one team, but too small to support two teams. Professor H. G. Demmert[1] suggests that this difficulty might be overcome by a rule specifying that a club in such a situation should play its home games at more than one venue, as occurs in American basketball, though this may not work where transport facilities are good. This practice is also common in English county cricket, although the reason here seems to be a desire to give more people the opportunity of seeing cricket of this quality rather than any notion of equalising competition. Another solution is to divide the league into divisions in the belief that clubs with access to large populations will predominate in the higher ones, as in English and Scottish League Football and the Major and Minor Counties arrangement in cricket.

[1] *The Economics of Professional Team Sports,* D. C. Heath & Co., Lexington, Mass., 1973.

Playing success stimulates attendance

A second factor determining attendance is playing success, which itself may partly be determined by population. In statistical studies a number of formulae have been used for playing success, such as total points gained over the season or percentage of games won. It is also possible that expectations of success are governed by previous performances. Some studies have tried to capture this effect by including variables such as success over five years measured in total points or in winning a trophy over four years. It is also likely that some fans are attracted by particular players. Variables such as the number of star players in a team, estimated on subjective judgement, have also been included in statistical analyses. Generally, it has been found that quality has a favourable independent effect on attendance.

Is price (adjusted by quality) significant?

A range of other variables has been used to explain variations in attendance. We would expect the price of admission to play some part in determining attendance, but it would perhaps be more appropriate to consider price adjusted for quality (II (*b*), p. 24). Failure to do this may explain why price has generally been found to be insignificant. Price competition is limited not only because each club has a local monopoly, but also because the league organisation may fix a standard or minimum price. Thus, in the English Football League, the league body determines a minimum price regardless of the division in which the team plays. Higher prices are charged for superior positions in the ground, so that one should include a variable such as proportion of seats to ground capacity or age of stadium.

Income per head in a locality may also be important in some sports. Thus, it has been found in American baseball that there is a significant inverse relationship between *per capita* income and attendance, whilst in basketball, in contrast, there is a significant direct relationship between them. Other variables which may be relevant, but are perhaps more difficult to incorporate into a statistical analysis of attendances, are the number of substitutes (the most obvious of which will be other professional sports, though their effect is often diminished because the seasons cover different parts of the year), the

[29]

style of play (whether attacking or defensive), the propensity to crowd violence or misbehaviour, the marketing of the game through advertisements or the media, the weather, and the time and date of the fixture.

Can 'uncertainty of outcome' be measured?

This leaves for consideration the question of how to incorporate uncertainty of outcome into the analysis. Closeness of competition is particularly difficult to capture statistically because of its variations during the season. Thus, that a team has a large lead at the beginning of the season may not depress attendances very much because spectators believe it may eventually be overtaken; late in the season the lead may mean that the contest is virtually over. This problem, rather than the unimportance of uncertainty of outcome, may explain why such variables have sometimes proved to be insignificant.[1] Messrs. R. A. Hart *et al.*,[2] in the only statistical analysis of English Football League attendances, estimate the total attendance at each match from league position of home and away team before the match, but with inconclusive results. Professors J. W. Hunt and K. A. Lewis,[3] in contrast, giving games behind at the end of the season twice the weight of those early in the season, found significant results. Professor R. G. Noll[4] tried several variables to represent closeness of competition in various North American sports, including average differences in winning percentages of first- and second-placed teams and number of winning games behind of the second-placed team. These differences were found to be important in baseball and ice-hockey, but not in football and basketball, where he suggested that the end-of-season play-off and the small number

[1] The crucial importance of uncertainty of outcome is illustrated by attendances at end-of-season soccer games. Towards the end of the 1978-79 season attendances at Queen's Park Rangers, relegated from the First Division of the Football League, fell below 10,000 compared with over 20,000 earlier. In Scotland, Rangers recorded two home attendances of 3,000 after they had lost the League to Celtic, although they ended the season as runners-up and won the other two major trophies.

[2] R. A. Hart, J. Hutton and T. Sharot, 'A Statistical Analysis of Association Football Attendances', *Journal of the Royal Statistical Society*, Series C, Vol. 24, No. 1, 1975.

[3] 'Dominance, Recontracting and the Reserve Clause: Major League Baseball', *American Economic Review*, Vol. 66, No. 5, 1976.

[4] (Ed.), *Government and the Sports Business,* Studies in the Regulation of Economic Activity, The Brookings Institution, Washington DC, 1974.

of teams in each division reduced the importance of this variable. Professor Demmert[1] also found in baseball that there was a significant direct relation between the average lead of a first-placed team and attendance, both in combined and in National League samples.

In short, this demand for tickets at the games of the leading club appears to go up rather than down as its lead over the second club increases. Closeness of competition only benefits the other clubs still contending for the title. These studies indicate how difficult it is to make adequate allowance for uncertainty of outcome in statistical analyses.

Are some teams unduly dominant?

Adopting a rather different approach, Professors Hunt and Lewis attempted to measure the effects of dominance (measured in the percentage of games won by the team in the city with the largest population) in one baseball division of six teams over five seasons.[2] The results indicated that total revenue for the division as a whole was maximised when the large city team won 43 per cent of the time, that the revenue of the remaining divisional teams was maximised when the large city team won 20 per cent of the time, and that the revenue of the large city team itself was maximised when it won 80 per cent of the time. This result indicated, therefore, the inherent conflict between the interests of the individual club and that of the league as a whole.

(d) The motivation of club owners and controllers
(i) Profit?

Given that uncertainty of outcome is an important determinant of attendance and hence revenue, how will it influence the behaviour of the participants? As a starting point one might, following Professor Rottenberg, assume that club controllers attempt to maximise their profits. Any de-stabilising effects of imbalance in market power might then eventually be rectified by competition. If one or two clubs begin to dominate the league, the purchase of additional players by them (or replacement of existing players by superior ones) will eventually increase total revenue at a decreasing rate (or even begin to

---

[1] *Op. cit.*

[2] Unfortunately, there is no comparable analysis of British sports.

reduce it). The *law of diminishing returns** is applicable here, as elsewhere, and profits may fall, even if playing success continues to rise. The implication for the profit-maximising club is that it should sell some of its players to other clubs, so that it becomes less successful and its opponents more so in terms of playing success, with increased profits for all the clubs as a consequence of more uncertainty of outcome. (Further analysis of this point is in V(i), pp. 64-66.)

(ii) *Prestige?*

The traditional theory of the firm assumed that entrepreneurs attempt to maximise their profits. Recent theorising has suggested alternative *maximands** such as sales, growth, wealth, prestige or utility. To the extent that controllers of clubs are wealthy sportsmen-owners who treat sporting activity as a form of consumption from which non-pecuniary rather than monetary income is obtained,[1] it may be appropriate to explain the behaviour of clubs in terms of utility[2] (general level of satisfaction) rather than profit maximisation. Quite different predictions might follow.

At the extreme, the objective may then be to maximise the number of games won regardless of financial constraints. But a more realistic assumption is the maximisation of games won subject to a minimum profit (or maximum loss).[3] The prediction would then be that only minimum profits will be earned

[1] Pure profit-maximising behaviour may not meet with the whole-hearted approval of the spectator. Thus, as one American sports arbitrator suggests: 'The faithful adherence of the fans to the fate of a club and the interest of the public is based upon their conception of basketball, baseball, football, hockey and tennis as competitive games in which the contests are carried on under a code of fair and just practices and with recognition of the virtues which an earlier public perceived in amateur sports. If baseball, for example, is conceived by the public only as a commercial enterprise its rapture is not for long.' (Peter Seitz, 'Are Professional Sports Sports or Business? Or How Much Would You Pay for Catfish Hunter?', in J. L. Stern and Barbara B. Dennis, (eds.), *Industrial Relations Research Association 1976 Proceedings*, University of Wisconsin, 1977.)

[2] P. J. Sloane, 'The Economics of Professional Football: The Football Club as a Utility Maximiser', *Scottish Journal of Political Economy*, Vol. XVII, No. 2, June 1971.

[3] Even prestige can be bought at too high a price as the costs of sustaining it will be determined by the market in the long run. Thus 'Some people honestly say they run a business for the fun of it, as is sometimes contended by owners of racing stables and professional athletic teams. Still, the higher the costs of that activity in terms of losses of wealth, the less likely will that hobby be sustained.' (A. A. Alchian and W. R. Allen, *University Economics: Elements of Inquiry*, 3rd Edn., Wadsworth, California, 1972, p. 127.)

where there are opportunities for strengthening a team. In either case clubs would not sell players merely to increase their profits as implied by profit maximisation. Further, it would appear that unrestrained attempts to maximise the number of games won, where clubs vary in their ability to draw fans, would lead to financial ruin in the absence of restrictive rules, such as on clubs' property rights over players. Even constrained maximisation of games won will result in more inequality of playing performance than where profit-maximising objectives are followed.

Such a mixture of objectives may also have implications for the size of sporting leagues. Assuming that profitability falls as the size of league increases, which would seem to follow if additional entrants have smaller 'gates' from smaller populations, average size will be larger if the purpose is to maximise games won rather than profits. On the other hand, additional clubs may not be welcomed into the league, since this may reduce the probability of winning for existing league members. Certainly, where club owners are motivated by playing success rather than profit maximisation, the degree of inequality is likely to be wider and the pressure for collective action by the league to moderate financial advantages of one club over another will be increased.

This conclusion raises the intriguing possibility that the interests of consumers as a whole might be better served if club owners acted as pure profit-maximisers rather than trying to achieve playing success to satisfy a wider range of motives. Such behaviour is likely to be unacceptable to the fans of any one club, who wish to see their club win. Further, the result of aiming at pure profit maximisation would appear to be a smaller number of clubs and some loss of consumer welfare in areas not represented in the league as a consequence: some spectators in smaller towns will be deprived of the opportunity of seeing their local team compete in the league.

(iii) *The profitability of professional team sports*

There is no consensus among economists on which motive—profit or prestige—is more appropriate in professional team sports. The North American literature has emphasised profit maximisation on the ground that there is no evidence that sportsmen-owners have received other than a market return on their investment. Indeed, unlike team sports in Britain, American team sports generally appear to be extremely profitable.[1] It may be significant that, in the various leagues, the number of clubs tends to be smaller in the US than in European team sports, although population is much larger in the US than in any Western European country. Further, in American sports each of the major leagues has had periods of expansion, contraction and the movement of franchises (the right to locate a club in a particular city) away from cities with small crowd potential to ones with more potential. In Europe such examples are rare and there is no equivalent of the franchise system or competition between leagues in the same sport.

Long-run losses in European sports

British and other European experience is thus quite different from that of US sports. In many sports, clubs make long-run losses from sporting activities and remain in business only through donations from wealthy businessmen on the boards of directors or through income from non-sporting activities. In the English Football League the rules even forbid payments for directors' services; and there is a limitation on the payment of dividends to shareholders. A survey by the Commission on Industrial Relations[2] found that from 1968 to 1973 49 (out of 92) Football League clubs from which information was obtained lost a total of £1,744,900, including revenue from sources other than gate receipts.

In cricket, non-commercial aspects are even more marked, with nearly all counties being loss-making.[3] Three-day county cricket attracts few spectators, but is defended on the ground, amongst others, that it is necessary to produce players of Test-match calibre (i.e. an investment). The financial survival of county cricket is at least partly dependent on the revenue

[continued on p. 38]

[1] Noll, *op. cit.*

[2] Report No. 87, *Professional Football*, HMSO, 1974.

[3] D. White, 'Is County Cricket Dying', *New Society*, 22 June 1978, reports that Leicestershire County Cricket Club has returned a profit for nine consecutive years, a record for the 17 first-class counties. Here again, however, income from normal sources such as membership subscriptions, gate money and television, etc., is only £100,000 per annum against an expenditure of £200,000. The difference is accounted for by income obtained from a lottery. The Secretary of the club is reported as saying that 'balancing the books is as important as winning games'.

TABLE II

UNPROFITABILITY OF CRICKET AS MEASURED BY SPECTATOR PAYMENTS:

Income and Expenditure Accounts for Two County Cricket Clubs, 1977 and 1978

INCOME (£000's)

	Kent		Sussex	
	1977	*1978*	*1977*	*1978*
Subscriptions (membership)	65·5	84·6	45·2	42·9
Donations	5·8	18·4	4·0	3·0
Gate receipts from spectators	48·6	68·8	18·3	13·4
Share of sponsored competition income and royalties	35·4	62·6	24·4	42·8
Other income	24·6	33·5	30·6	29·1
TOTAL INCOME	180·0	267·8	122·4	141·2
Balance (Loss)	(32·0)	(35·3)	(59·5)	(72·8)
	212·0	303·1	181·9	214·1
Extraneous income, supporters' club donations and fund raising, etc.	18·3	69·8	14·2	9·8
Share of Test matches and tours	34·7	36·4	44·2	27·9
Loss provision for share of legal costs in Packer case	—	(9·7)	(9·2)	—
Taxation (paid or reclaimed)	(2·8)	(9·7)	0·4	—
Surplus (Deficit)	18·1	51·5	(10·0)	(35·1)

EXPENDITURE (£000's)

	Kent		Sussex	
Administration expenses	43·6	73·0	42·0	45·1
Cricket staff	68·2	97·8	58·7	79·3
Match expenses	44·1	58·3	37·7	51·6
Ground maintenance	39·5	44·3	37·8	29·8
Other	16·6	29·6	5·6	8·2
TOTAL EXPENDITURE	212·0	303·1	181·9	214·1

Source: Kent County Cricket Club *Reports and Accounts 1978*; Sussex County Cricket Club *Report and Accounts for the Year 1977/78.*

[35]

CONSEQUENCES

The importance of the argument for British readers

1 SPECTATORS

(i) Since spectator interest is enhanced the higher is the uncertainty of outcome of games, sports league cartels benefit the spectator by ensuring that competing teams are more equally matched.

(ii) In redistributing revenue among member clubs, restricting price competition between them, and circumscribing their property rights in players, league organisations widen consumer choice by maintaining in existence more clubs than would otherwise survive.

(iii) League cartels, however, also encourage inefficiencies in the marketing of sports and retard innovations which would attract larger numbers of spectators.

(iv) The Kerry Packer initiative in cricket and other entrepreneurial challenges to the established sporting authorities have demonstrated the value of competition in initiating reforms which provide the spectator with more interesting entertainment and more congenial facilities at sports grounds.

2 PLAYERS

(i) Since players are concerned to maximise their income over a relatively short career, the recent easing of restrictions on player mobility and the marketing innovations introduced by private sponsors of competing leagues and tournaments have helped by raising the real incomes of players in several sports.

(ii) Although the highest rewards have gone to individuals with exceptional talent, players generally have gained from the higher revenues attracted to the sports.

3 CLUBS

(i) Despite the activities of league cartels in redistributing income among clubs and limiting competition between them, many clubs in several professional sports face severe financial difficulties which make it doubtful whether the major professional team sports in Britain can continue to operate with the present number of clubs at the top.

(ii) If the heavier financial costs resulting from increased player mobility are to be met, clubs will need to be more enterprising in identifying and exploiting the scope for attracting more spectators and sponsors.

(iii) The incentive to become more enterprising, however, is probably blunted by the weakness of property rights in the ownership of British sports clubs and the absence of profit motivation.

4 LEAGUE ORGANISATIONS

(i) Where professional sports leagues have been notably unimaginative in devising new methods to attract more resources into their sports, competition from new entrepreneurs has highlighted the scope for increasing spectator interest and sponsorship, for maximising income from television and the other media, and for attracting new categories of spectator.

(ii) Though sports leagues could usefully devote more attention to revenue-sharing arrangements to ensure sporting equality, they will more effectively promote the welfare of member clubs by encouraging enterprise and innovation in marketing so as to enlarge total revenue.

5 GOVERNMENT

(i) Professional sports possess features which set them apart from other industries. Most notably, the firms (clubs) in the industry are mutually dependent, their output being in the nature of a joint product (the game).

(ii) It may consequently be necessary for government to recognise professional team sports as a special case of competition and continue to allow partial exemptions from monopoly and restrictive practices legislation.

(iii) This privilege must not be permitted to foster inefficient practices. The maintenance of 'workable competition' is important in promoting innovation and entrepreneurship.

(iv) So long as the sports industry remains open to potential competitors, government prohibition of non-competitive practices in general may yield small social gains but cause significant social losses.

received by the counties as their share of Test-match receipts. Table II (p. 35) presents details of income and expenditure in comparable form for two of the more successful counties—Kent and Sussex. In 1977 Kent shared the Schweppes County Championship (with Middlesex) and in 1978 won it outright, together with the Benson and Hedges Cup; Sussex were winners of the Gillette Cup in 1978. Neither, however, was able to cover its expenditure from its cricket revenue, though Kent was just viable when income received as its share of Test matches and tours is included.[1] The small revenue received from gate receipts reflects the low takings at three-day county games, receipts from other games (apart from the preliminary matches of the Benson and Hedges Cup Competition) being pooled and shared equally among all counties. Kent's relatively healthy financial position owes much to a recently introduced pool and lottery which raised over £43,000 in 1978.

A lack of commercial awareness may derive from the concern with playing success rather than profitability of the committees which run the cricket counties or the managers who run soccer clubs or other sports. In turn this unconcern with profit may be explained as a consequence of sportsmen-owners' weak or non-existent property rights in sports clubs and league organisations. In England, Football Association rules prohibit payment to directors, and all but one club (Nottingham Forest) are private limited liability companies with restrictions on the transferability of shares. The two basic elements of private property, exclusivity and transferability of rights, are weaker, so that the sports club is in this sense a non-profit enterprise. Further, managers are frequently former players who, given a choice, may be expected to give more attention to playing success than to maximisation of profits. Given that price setting requires time and effort, there will be little incentive to search for the optimal price which maximises income from gate receipts or optimal subscriptions, or the optimal combination of gate receipts from a single game and subscriptions for a season (further discussed in pp. 42-43). Price may, therefore, be set too low.

[1] In 1977 the Test and County Cricket Board (TCCB) distributed £1·5 million to the counties comprising income from the Australian Test series, sponsorship and fees. In total this was estimated to be equivalent to half the income the counties required to break even. In 1978 the surplus amounted to approximately £1·2 million, or 30 per cent of the break-even income. Counties which staged Test matches received about £69,000 and the remainder £53,000 each.

Black market in Cup Final tickets: prices too low—a neglect of property rights?

This aspect of the market for sport can be illustrated by the demand for Cup Final tickets, which always outstrips supply at the price set by the Football Association (FA). The resulting flourishing black market in such tickets sends prices as high as 10 times their official face value. The FA has gone to elaborate lengths (but has failed) to prevent the resale of tickets at higher prices by attempting to trace the origin of black market tickets in relation to their allocation to member clubs.

Professors Alchian and Allen[1] point to a similar occurrence in the annual Rose Bowl Football Game in California. There, the association which puts on the event is not, as with professional sports clubs in the USA, privately owned in the conventional sense, but a body designed to support participating universities financially, so that there is no direct financial interest for the members of the association. In such circumstances, the decision-makers will maximise utility by setting price too low, since prestige is enhanced by the ability to provide tickets in excess demand to friends and relatives, particularly for the most expensive seats. Also there will be a desire to avoid setting prices so high that some seats remain unsold to the detriment of the occasion. If there were private property rights we would expect the owners of such facilities to fix prices so that they more closely equated supply and demand and thus maximised profits.

The entry of Kerry Packer into international cricket is relevant in the context of property rights. It may be seen as an attack by a profit-maximising entrepreneur on a utility-maximising establishment that sets winning or prestige above the aim of covering costs and maximising profit. Thus Messrs P. S. Wilson and R. H. Allan, two economists at the University of Melbourne, have argued:

'Prior to the formation of World Series Cricket, the Australian Cricket Board operated as a monopolist/monopsonist in international cricket in Australia. Its basic aim was to provide as high a standard of cricket as possible, rather than to maximise the financial return on any series. Its major financial constraint was to cover expenses and to provide subsidies for lower levels of cricketing competition. Thus its rôle was essentially that of a utility-maximiser. The entry of World Series Cricket changed

[1] *Op. cit.*, pp. 145-46.

the industrial structure to that of a *duopoly/duopsony*,* with a profit-maximiser challenging the position of the utility-maximiser —with far-reaching effects on the structure of competition.'[1]

To maximise revenues it was necessary for WSC not only to recruit high-quality players but also to ensure they were distributed more or less equally among the three teams—WSC Australians, WSC West Indians and the Rest of the World—to ensure uncertainty of outcome. Wilson and Allan find there was no significant difference in the batting and bowling abilities of any pair of the three WSC squads. Thus, WSC's allocation of players had established teams of roughly equal quality to maximise uncertainty of outcome, the means to the object of profit maximisation. The impact of WSC on established cricket competitions is examined in detail in IV *(b)* (pp. 58-63).

(e) Sporting leagues as cartels

So much for the economic (or non-economic) behaviour of individual clubs. We now examine their group behaviour as members of a league. The major issues to be determined by the sporting cartel are the number of producers or the size of league, the location of production, the allocation of playing resources, admission prices and revenue-sharing arrangements. League organisations may also negotiate for member clubs with TV companies, pools promoters and industrial sponsors. Industry cartelisation is generally a response to an oligopolistic market structure, in which one firm's price/output decision will affect the market position of other firms because numbers are few. In the sports industry, cartelisation in the form of the league is necessary for there to be a viable product at all. This may mean that sporting cartels are rather more stable than industrial cartels, since no club can continue to produce output outside the league unless it joins another cartel (i.e. a competing league). Nor is there the same danger from price-cutting or increased output in the sporting cartel, since each club has a spatial monopoly.

Cartel 'cheating'

It does not follow there are no differences of interest among the member clubs. Presumably the large city clubs would

---

[1] P. S. Wilson and R. H. Allan, 'The Economics of International Cricket in Australia', paper presented at the 7th Conference of Economists, MacQuarie University, 28 August-1 September 1978.

prefer a rather less equal division of gate receipts to enhance their probability of winning, the smaller clubs a more equal division.[1] Where opportunities arise member clubs may attempt to 'cheat' in order to gain an advantage over the other members of the league by paying bonuses or approaching players of other clubs outside the rules.

Following the assumption that individual clubs try to maximise their profits, North American economists have suggested that the objective of the league is the maximisation of the joint profit of its members. Professor J. C. H. Jones[2] argues that, when it is recognised that there are conflicts between optimum league and individual club objectives, 'constrained' profit maximisation, i.e. profits compatible with the survival of the league, will follow. Yet a club's potential return from fielding a winning team may exceed its potential loss from reduced uncertainty of outcome. Most of the costs of the latter may be borne by other member clubs. If so, rational behaviour will cause individual clubs to improve the quality of their players beyond the degree optimal for the league as a whole.[3]

'Satisfactory' rather than (short-run) maximum profits

In this situation the pursuit of a 'satisfactory' amount of profits rather than the maximum (at least in the short run) may be the outcome. This policy is likely to be reinforced where playing success in a league is a qualification for other lucrative

---

[1] The outcome will be determined by voting power. In the English Football League, for instance, each of the 44 clubs in the First and Second Divisions is entitled to one vote at the annual general meeting. The 48 clubs of the Third and Fourth Divisions are only associate members and cannot vote individually except with the consent of the full members. At general meetings the associate members are represented by four delegates with full voting powers. Changes in the regulations require the support of three-quarters of those present and entitled to vote, which tends to assist in the preservation of the *status quo*. At the limits it will be necessary for the cartel to adopt policies which do not give the stronger clubs an incentive to break away to form a super league and the desired number of weaker clubs the incentive to leave the major leagues to enter minor leagues, where not only income potential but also costs are lower.

[2] 'The Economics of the National Hockey League', *Canadian Journal of Economics*, February 1969.

[3] Demmert, *op. cit.* The club and its supporters will want to win individual games by the highest possible margin, but presumably the satisfaction obtained would be more where a big win was obtained over a more successful team. One might also distinguish between the 'hard-core' supporters who want to maximise success and the more 'marginal' supporters who are attracted by uncertainty of outcome.

competitions, as in the international club competitions of European soccer. These represent a major source of instability, since success in the home competition may not guarantee success in international competitions, and there is consequently an inducement for clubs to become very much stronger than other clubs in their national league.

On practical grounds, doubt is therefore cast on Professor Rottenberg's assumption that the goal of profit maximisation is itself sufficient to ensure that sporting competition does not become too unequal. Indeed, for the health of domestic competitions it might even be preferable to exclude clubs that compete in international competitions permanently. If joint profit maximisation were the objective of the league organisation, rules should be organised to facilitate above-average wins for large city teams and below-average wins for small town teams in order to maximise total attendances. In such a market the increased attendances in the large cities would outweigh the reduced attendances in the small towns. A league organisation that was predominantly interested in the health of the league or sporting competition would, on the other hand, adopt policies resulting in more equality of performance. Similarly, league bodies concerned with the well-being of the game may prefer large leagues in order to spread the game to as many towns as possible.

Profit maximisation may dictate, in contrast, a relatively small league to minimise cross-subsidisation (covering losses in 'uneconomic' clubs by transfers of revenues from profitable ones). The smaller the league, however, the fewer the number of games and the more the need to offset this loss by additional tournaments (or, as in the Scottish Football League, by arranging that teams play each other four times rather than twice a season). Optimal league size may then be considered to be that number of clubs (and subsequent games) which maximises total revenue, subject to all clubs being more or less viable. As suggested earlier (p. 33), the relatively large size of British and other European leagues suggests non-profit-maximising behaviour.

(i) Cartel pricing policy

To achieve sporting equality the pricing policy of the cartel should be directed towards ensuring, as far as possible, that revenues are equalised for member clubs. In British team sports like soccer there has been a tendency to fix common admission prices regardless of the status of the club or the division in which it plays. It does not necessarily follow that common prices will equalise income, for *elasticity of demand** may differ, so that the aim of equal revenue implies that clubs should charge *different* prices. If a club faced a relatively elastic demand curve, a lower price might enlarge total revenue; another club with a relatively inelastic demand curve would achieve the same result with a higher price.

In major games such as the FA Cup Final or Test matches between Australia and England the size of stadium is always, or often, inadequate to meet the demand. As in the individual club (p. 38), 'black markets' in tickets for such games point to the failure to use price as a rationing device. Whilst care has to be taken to avoid loss of consumer goodwill, the authorities have frequently shown a lack of awareness of the significance of demand elasticities, or perhaps a disinclination to search for optimal prices in the absence of well-defined property rights. County cricket clubs have, for instance, been loathe to raise their annual subscriptions for fear of losing members. It is, however, possible that members, being the hard core of the supporters, have a relatively inelastic demand for the product, so that a fall in members would be more than compensated for by the higher prices. Table II, which shows that subscriptions brought in more income than gate receipts in both Kent and Sussex (although paying at the gate commits supporters to watch only one game, whilst membership implies attendance at several games to obtain a saving), points perhaps to some substitution of membership for paying at the gate. That is, membership may be too cheap relative to the price of admission.

(ii) *External sources of revenue*

External sources of revenue present a particular threat to the equalisation policy of the cartel, since they may be harder to control than admission prices. TV and broadcasting rights, for instance, are an important potential source of revenue. The common practice is for the league organisation to negotiate TV contracts and pools revenue in soccer for the member clubs and to share the revenues equally amongst them. The problem is more acute when the external sources of finance take different forms with particular clubs. Sponsors may choose

[43]

to subsidise more successful rather than less successful clubs, through advertising and other means, and this source of income may be more difficult to pool. Monopoly rights over the sale of games for TV viewing put the league organisation in a strong position to negotiate a high price, as well as raising issues of public policy, such as whether there is a conflict with monopolies and restrictive practices legislation. There is also the question of whether TV viewers bear their (market) share of the cost of producing the sports they watch.

The Football League, LWT and the BBC

In November 1978 the Football League attempted to make a £4·9 million exclusive agreement with London Weekend Television (LWT) for recording League matches. The BBC issued High Court writs against both LWT and the Football League, seeking to obtain a declaration that LWT was bound by an agreement to negotiate jointly with the BBC, and an injunction to prevent the League and LWT from putting their agreement into effect. The Director-General of the Office of Fair Trading examined the agreement on the grounds that it was, *prima facie*, contrary to the restrictive practices legislation.

Subsequently, the Football League signed a four-year contract jointly with the BBC and ITV for £9·2 million, with an extra £800,000 for overseas film sales, including limited built-in guarantees against inflation of 10 per cent for each of the four years. This agreement will provide each of the 92 League clubs with an income of £25,000 per year from TV and represents a considerable increase over the old agreement worth only £1·5 million over three years. The agreement was ratified by the clubs only after considerable debate, many clubs arguing that the product had been sold too cheaply to the TV companies.

One factor inducing acceptance was that without a TV agreement the clubs would lose additional income from advertising hoardings at grounds, but considerable controversy remains over whether TV, through its exposure of the game, increases or reduces attendances. The agreement specifies that the two networks will take it in turns to screen League football on Saturday nights and Sunday afternoons. The BBC and ITV have also agreed to alternate the screening of the 1980 Olympics and the 1982 World Cup. This is a rare example of a restrictive agreement increasing consumer choice, though perhaps at the cost of reduced quality of presentation.

Packer's 'Channel Nine' TV network v. the Australian Broadcasting Commission

The main reason for Kerry Packer's entry into cricket was his desire to obtain exclusive rights to the lucrative televising of Test matches when the existing agreement with the Australian Broadcasting Commission (ABC) expired early in 1979. When the International Cricket Conference (ICC) refused this request, Packer's response was to form his own Test series to televise the games on his 'Channel Nine' network.

Subsequently, after the settlement between Packer and the Australian Cricket Board and the attainment of exclusive TV rights (outlined on p. 62), the ABC sought on 2 January 1980 an interim injunction restraining the Cricket Board of Control and Packer's Channel 9 from televising cricket exclusively. This request was rejected in the Federal Court, as was the ABC's subsequent application (12 February 1980) for a permanent injunction. A further appeal by the ABC is pending.

Cricket sponsorship: to raise quality, not achieve equality

The expansion of sponsorship in cricket has become an increasingly significant source of income (as is true of many other sports). In 1979 Cornhill Insurance sponsored the Test series against India for £175,000 and Prudential provided £22,300 for the one-day World Cup series. Schweppes have re-negotiated sponsorship of the County Championship (but only for one year) following the expiry in 1979 of the three-year £400,000 agreement. Benson and Hedges provide £130,000 for their Cup competition; comparable sums are provided by John Player and Gillette for the competitions bearing their names.

The way in which these sums are allocated is designed to achieve not playing equality but playing quality as seen by spectators, since the larger sums are paid as a reward for winning. In the Schweppes competition in 1979, the winning county (Essex) received £8,000, the second £3,500 and the third £1,750; £120 was provided for every win and £5 for every batting and bowling bonus point. (Similar incentives apply in other sponsorships.) Whilst the ability of the richer

[45]

counties to attract the star players is restricted by birth and residential rules, these inducements must increase their chances of obtaining the top foreign players (unless signing foreign players is banned). In general, there are advantages in ensuring that all sponsorship arrangements are channelled through the league organisation as a whole rather than negotiated individually by the clubs themselves in order to ensure uncertainty of outcome, though this restriction of competition will intensify the degree of cartelisation.

(iii) *Division of gate receipts between home and away clubs*

A crucial policy issue for the league cartel is the division of gate receipts between the home and away clubs and the proportion to be pooled and shared equally among all members of the league. The diversity of arrangements in the various sports, ranging from all the receipts to the home side in the County Cricket Championship and speedway to a 50/50 share in the Scottish Football League and the Rugby League (with a 15 per cent pool in the latter), suggests that the income-equalising potential of gate-sharing arrangements has not been fully appreciated or perhaps has been resisted by the larger clubs for whom it would mean a loss of revenue.[1]

The effect of a more even revenue split is to make more clubs viable. Thus in baseball Professors Hunt and Lewis[2] estimate that an increase in the gate share of the away team from 20 per cent to 50 per cent would result in a gain of £1 million to all teams but the dominant one (and a corresponding loss to the latter). To encourage more uncertainty of outcome, therefore, several economists have proposed that there should be a more equal division of gate receipts. One example is 50 per cent to the home team, 25 per cent to the away team and 25 per cent to a pool.[3] The most extreme proposal is that *all* gate receipts should be pooled and divided equally among the clubs, thereby eliminating any problems that might result from inequalities in population potential.[4]

---

[1] I discuss income-sharing arrangements in UK and North America sports more fully in the *Bulletin of Economic Research*, Vol. 28, No. 1, May 1976.

[2] *Op. cit.*

[3] Noll, *op. cit.*

[4] B. Dabscheck, 'Sporting Equality: Labour Market *vs* Product Market Control', *Journal of Industrial Relations,* June 1975, and the comment by P. J. Sloane, *ibid.,* March 1976.

Profit maximisation would seem to rule out this proposal, since it would remove the incentive to win. Each club would concentrate on minimising costs in order to raise profits, thereby diminishing the quality of playing performance and increasing inefficiency.

Where clubs attempted to maximise playing success these issues would be less crucial, even if a smaller surplus over costs is implied. But there are still some difficulties:

(i) Control of all gate receipts and their distribution by the league may give rise to doubts in the public's mind about the independence of clubs and possibly even the honesty of contests.

(ii) The larger clubs would be bound to resist, since the effect of such a policy would be to reduce not only their revenue but their probability of winning.

(iii) The ability of league clubs to compete at international level would be threatened.

(iv) The wealthier clubs might break away to form their own league.

It is doubtful, therefore, whether centralised control and equal allocation of gate receipts is a practicable policy, although, as suggested in the conclusions (VI, 5), there are strong arguments in favour of a more equal division of receipts. The argument for reform has become more marked with the weakening of labour market control (IV *(a)*, pp. 53-58).

Summary of conditions for uncertainty of outcome

A league cartel desiring to achieve uncertainty of outcome should

(i) ensure as far as possible that the geographical location of clubs minimises differences in population potential;

(ii) set prices in such a way as to minimise income difference between clubs;

(iii) pool a proportion of league income to maintain the viability of the weaker clubs; and

(iv) control the allocation of playing talent among the clubs (III).

The wider the inequalities among clubs the more difficult it will be to achieve these objectives, and the more the danger that some will try to form a new league with similarly placed clubs.

[47]

III. THE LABOUR MARKET

(a) Monopsonistic rules

The labour market in professional team sports is a classic case of *monopsony*,* in which a single buyer faces competing suppliers, since there is no comparable alternative source of employment for the professional player other than the sports league which employs him. Rules limiting player mobility between clubs mean that once a player is contracted to a club he is in practice in a labour market separate from that of other clubs.[1] The rules are imposed by agreement among clubs in all professional team sports.

(i) Controls on entry

The entry of players into a sport may be controlled by rules on place of birth or residence. In English county cricket the governing body does not normally allow the registration of a player born outside the county unless or until he has met specified residential qualifications. These rules have been modified to allow the import of a limited number of foreign players to raise the quality of performance (e.g. each English cricket county is allowed up to two overseas players). In the Victorian Football League in Australia, players are zoned according to their place of birth and can move to another club (zone) only by remaining out of the game for three years.[2]

In theory such rules on entry, if rigidly enforced, could obviate alternative restrictive arrangements designed to achieve sporting equality. They change the nature of territorial competition from skills in players to entrepreneurship in the managers. Where the areas or zones as in English county cricket vary widely in population, one type of inequality (in playing talent) may be substituted for another (in income potential), and even areas of equal population would not ensure that an equal number of star players emerged in each.

[1] P. J. Sloane, 'The Labour Market in Professional Football', *British Journal of Industrial Relations*, Vol. VII, No. 2, 1969.

[2] A full description is in B. Dabscheck, 'The Wage Determination Process for Sportsmen', *Economic Record* (Melbourne), March 1975.

A second approach to limiting freedom of entry is the annual player draft, as in the four major North American team sports. Teams select, at a specified time each year, amateur sportsmen to add to their list of players, usually selected in reverse order of their positions in the league at the end of the previous season. Thus, the weaker teams have first choice of the potentially superior players who can negotiate only with the team that has selected them (in baseball an unsigned player may return to the draft after six months). Doubts have been expressed about the ability of the player draft to improve the weaker teams in a sufficiently short period to reduce inequality to acceptable degrees.[1] There would nevertheless be advantages in alternative systems that, say, permitted the clubs to select more than one player in sequence in each round; such arrangements might be contemplated by British team sports.

A third means of controlling entry is to limit the number of players a club may retain at any one time, as in baseball, ice-hockey and rugby league. This method is not adequate to ensure playing equality even where maintained at a relatively low figure, given substantial variations in skill among players. Obviously, a movement towards freedom of contract for established players would make the rules on entry more crucial.

(ii) *Mobility by transfer*

The second group of rules relates to the mobility of established players and incorporates the 'retain and transfer system' of soccer and the 'reserve clause' of baseball. Each of the American team sports has until very recently included a reserve clause which gives the team possessing a player's contract unfettered ownership of his services for the duration of his career or until the contract is sold to another club. In other sports this system has been modified by the ability to play out a contract—an additional year in American football (at 90 per cent of the previous salary) and basketball, or an extra three years in ice-hockey—to be free to negotiate with another team. Even under such circumstances, the owning club in American football and

---

[1] B. Price and A. G. Rao, 'Alternative Rules for Drafting in Professional Sports', in R. E. Machol, S. P. Ledany and D. G. Morrison (eds.), *Management Science in Sports*, North-Holland Publishing Co., Amsterdam, 1976.

ice-hockey must be compensated by cash, player exchanges or draft choices.

Before its recent amendment the retain-and-transfer system in British soccer was similar to the reserve clause, except that the contract specified an initial period (frequently one year) and an option period (equal to or less than the initial period). If a club failed to exercise its option, which had to grant the player terms no less favourable than the initial terms, he became a free agent. Otherwise, he might be transferred to another club only by mutual agreement, usually involving a transfer fee. In rugby league, clubs circulate each year a retained list of players and a list of those open to transfer at stipulated prices. In cricket there is no system of transfer fees, even where players are allowed to change counties after a qualifying period. This may be a consequence of the tradition of amateur or gentleman players and of the comparative rarity of transfers.

The most restrictive rules are those of baseball and British speedway, where the transfer of players or riders has not required their consent. These rules, which increase the (un-recorded) capital value of the clubs' assets, have come under attack from players' unions and interested parties not only on the grounds of unacceptability but also because of possible illegality if tested in the courts. It is unlikely that as much reliance as in the past can be placed on such restrictions.

(iii) *Limitations on payment*

The third method of reducing competition in the labour market is to limit the payment. In baseball in the 19th century, and until 1961 in English soccer, no club was permitted to pay more than a common maximum wage, a practice justified on the ground that it would give clubs an equal chance of attracting the best players. Such a rule persists in the Victorian Football League (Australian rules football) where there are fixed payments (minimum and maximum) based on the number of games played.

Despite penalty clauses, these rules are not rigidly enforced and have been moderated to permit additional payments.[1] Given the monopsony power of the employer and the 'monopoly' of player unions, the bargaining process in wage deter-

[1] Dabscheck, *op. cit.*

mination may seem to be bilateral monopoly. But collective bargaining in professional team sports tends to be concerned with fringe benefits and conditions of employment, whilst salaries (including bonuses) tend to be determined by negotiations between club and player.

(b) Exploitation of labour

Monopsonistic labour markets may give rise to 'exploitation', where labour is paid less than the value of its *marginal product**. Exploitation is quite consistent, therefore, with a market in which employees receive 'high' salaries, as in professional team sports. To estimate the extent of exploitation requires first of all the estimation of players' marginal revenue products (MRP). Such an attempt has been made in baseball,[1] though not in British sports. The procedure is to estimate, first, the relationship between performance and team wins (a 'production function') and, second, the effect of performance on revenue (a 'team revenue function'). Comparing the MRP estimates with player salaries, G. W. Scully found a considerable degree of exploitation.

More explicitly considered over career length, average baseball players appear to receive salaries at best equal to about 20 per cent of their MRPs. A smaller but still substantial amount of exploitation has been estimated by M. H. Medoff,[2] who found that hitters were paid between 30 and 41 per cent of their MRP (the latter figure relating to star players) and pitchers between 49 and 55 per cent.

The exploitation has been perpetuated by the three kinds of restrictive rules ((i), (ii) and (iii) above). In particular, the transfer fee in a competitive market would go to the player rather than the club that holds his contract. Unlike other sectors of the labour market, however, this may not increase significantly the quantity of labour supplied, since the supply of star players is inelastic.

Application of the economic analysis to British soccer and cricket

In theory it is possible to derive MRP estimates in other sports such as cricket, where data are available on run averages per

---

[1] G. W. Scully, 'Pay and Performance in Major League Baseball', *American Economic Review*, Vol. 64, December 1974.

[2] 'On Monopsonistic Exploitation in Professional Baseball', *Quarterly Review of Economics and Business*, Vol. 16, No. 2, 1976.

innings for batsmen and runs-per-wicket for bowlers. The lack of earnings data makes such a study difficult, apart from factors such as batting order, the run rate, dismissal of higher- or lower-order batsmen, and fielding ability. An attempt has been made by Messrs Wilson and Allan[1] to explain WSC batsmen's and bowlers' salaries in terms of variables measuring performance. Superstar status, simple career averages and age or Test experience seem to be the relevant factors. In sports such as soccer the problems of estimating MRP are very much larger, since the scoring and prevention of goals is much more dependent on team work, making it difficult, if not impossible, to estimate the precise contribution of each player.

Further, where club owners are concerned with playing success or utility maximisation rather than profit maximisation, it does not follow that players are exploited in general. Indeed, financial losses incurred in the long run by many clubs suggest that players may receive wages higher than the value of their MRP, though it is possible that some (e.g. star) players may be exploited. In such cases, therefore, the removal of the retention clause may diminish employment opportunities for the players. Where profits are maximised employment may increase as the removal of exploitation forces employers to operate closer to the competitive output.

---

[1] 'The Economics of International Cricket in Australia', *op. cit.*

IV. INCREASED COMPETITION IN SPORTS SERVICES AND LABOUR

Limitations on competition are the hallmark of professional team sports and apply both to the 'service' (game) and to the 'labour' (players), that is, to the factor and product markets. Indeed, it has been suggested that product market monopoly is essential for the maintenance of controls over labour mobility.[1] Competition between rival leagues in the product market and player movement between them would (in the absence of agreements to share players) thwart controls over the movement of players within a league designed to achieve uncertainty of results. Increased competition for players would also, it is argued, raise their earnings and, combined with reduced gate receipts arising from the entry of additional clubs, threaten the profitability of the leagues.

Two developments have weakened the existing anti-competitive rules of professional team sports. *First,* in the 1960s player associations were formed, or became more active, in North America, Europe and Australia. Following limited success in enforcing changes in players' contracts through the courts, the player associations focussed their efforts on reform through collective bargaining agreements, buttressed by favourable legal decisions and threats of strikes by players.[2] *Second,* in international cricket the monopoly control of the authorities was broken by the entry of Kerry Packer's World Series Cricket with long-run consequences that remain to be determined (discussed below, pp. 62-63, 67).

(a) Increased freedom in the player markets

Pressures for the reform of the labour market in professional team sports have in many countries intensified in recent years.

---

[1] M. L. Lagod, 'An Economic Analysis of Major League Baseball: Anti-Trust Exemption—Who Benefits?', paper presented at the first *World Congress of Sports Sciences,* University of Cordoba, Argentina, 4-11 July 1978.

[2] There is a full discussion in B. Dabscheck, 'Player Associations and Professional Team Sports', *ibid.,* 1978. There has never been a strong movement among the players' organisations for a completely free players' market. It has been thought that equality among clubs may require *some* limitation on the ability of the rich clubs to sign up all the star players.

In the USA restrictive labour rules in professional team sports have long been an issue in public policy. Indeed, baseball is unique in having its player reservation system specifically exempted from the anti-trust laws under a 1922 Supreme Court ruling[1] that it was not engaged in inter-state commerce; later court decisions have taken the failure of Congress to include baseball in anti-trust laws as an implied exemption. Other sports do not have a total exemption, but they have been able to secure legislative changes which exempt some of their operations from the Sherman Act.

Anti-trust legislation has never been an issue in British sporting activity. Services (and hence professional sports) were not included within the scope of the legislation until the Monopoly and Mergers Act of 1965, which specifically excluded employment of workers and their conditions of employment.[2] Most services were, however, brought within the ambit of the legislation by the Restrictive Trade Practices (Services) Order, 1976. Further, the Fair Trading Act 1973 permits the Secretary of State to refer restrictive labour practices to the Monopolies and Mergers Commission to establish whether or not they are against the public interest.[3] A defence against such a reference is that such practices are necessary, or are no more stringent than is necessary, for the efficient conduct of these activities. If public opinion were to move firmly against restrictions in the labour markets of professional team sports, government intervention through legislation or other means is a possibility.

In the USA government control of the sports industry has been discussed on several occasions, the most recent being a 1976 House Select Committee on Professional Sports concerned at the apparent instability of the industry. Whilst no further action has yet been taken, the Committee strongly recommended that a new committee be established to conduct further investigations into the requirement for special legislation governing professional sports. In the UK it is far from certain that such government involvement would be welcomed by the

---

[1] *Federal Baseball v. National League.* This case arose from the attempt of the new Federal League to break the product market monopoly of the National League. This 1922 decision was re-affirmed in *Flood v. Kuhn,* 1974.

[2] Presumably anti-competitive practices such as minimum price-fixing by the Football League might be found to be at variance with the Act.

[3] It is probable that the legislators had in mind here practices enforced by groups of workers rather than by employers.

governing bodies, the players or the consumers ('fans'). Changes in the labour market (outlined below) make such a possibility less likely.

Changes in employment contracts

Marked changes in employment contracts in soccer and the four major North American team sports (American football, baseball, ice-hockey and basketball) have been introduced in the last few years as a result of collective bargaining agreements. In general players now have the right to terminate employment with clubs at the end of their contract, although they are subject to compensation from the new clubs based upon a formula specific to each sport.[1]

In baseball there are limits on the number both of clubs with which a player can negotiate and of free agents who can be signed by a club. The club obtaining the services of the player must, depending on its final position in the previous year's league competition, compensate the other club with draft choices in the following year. Nevertheless, this agreement represents an important advance for the players.

In North American football a major bone of contention has been the so-called Rozelle Rule of 1963, which limited the freedom of a player to play out his option by allowing the League Commissioner, at his sole discretion,[2] to name and award to the former club one or more players of the acquiring club. Under a 1977 five-year collective agreement the option

---

[1] In baseball the changes followed a challenge to the reserve clause in 1975 by two players who claimed they should be regarded as free agents after a full year without having signed their contracts—a claim upheld in arbitration. Subsequently, the players' association and the owners signed experimentally the 1976-79 Basic Agreement, under which all players can become free agents after acquiring six years of major league service and every five years thereafter.

[2] Again, the Courts in *Kapp v. National Football League* (1974) and *Mackey v. National Football League* (1975) agreed with the players' contention that the primary purpose of the rule was to discourage players from playing out their options rather than, as alleged by the clubs, to maintain competitive balance, preserve fan interest, protect the integrity of the game against suspicion of cheating and stabilise the industry by preventing open bidding for players at the end of every season. Noll, *op. cit.*, points out that public confidence in the honesty of play might be adversely affected if it were known that, during the season, a player was negotiating with other clubs in contention for the title, since it would be possible for poor play on his part with his current club to influence the outcome of the championship. A full discussion is in T. J. Bergmann and J. W. Dworkin, 'Collective Bargaining v. the Rozelle Rule: An Analysis of Labour-Managed Relations in Professional Football', *Akron Business and Economic Review*, Vol. 9, No. 2, Summer 1978.

clause is limited to players with less than four years' service.[1] The Rozelle Rule was eliminated, but in its place a free agent's former club was to be allowed first refusal of the player's services if it matched the player's highest offer from other clubs, and a compensation formula was introduced based on the free-agent player's salary in the previous season and in the form of future draft choices from the acquiring club. These formulae bear some comparison to the changes being introduced in European soccer (below).

In Britain, pressure for footballers' freedom of contract was supported by the government-appointed Committee on Football[2] in 1968 and by the Commission on Industrial Relations (CIR)[3] in 1974. Both were broadly in favour of substituting fixed-term contracts of several years' duration for the retain-and-transfer system, though with transitional arrangements. Following discussions with the players' union (PFA), the Management Committee of the English Football League presented to member clubs in November 1975, proposals which allowed for a form of freedom of contract. To protect the weaker clubs financially from the loss of a player's services, there was to be a formula by which the new club would compensate the old, based on the player's annual salary and a multiplying factor governed by his age and the division of his former club. Compensation was to decline with age (in three groups: 18-24, 25-27 and 28-30) and to increase with the division in the league of the new club, the largest multiplying factor applying to the transfer of a player from the lowest (4th) division club to the highest (1st) division club. This formula represented a somewhat crude attempt to estimate the *marginal productivity** of players.

To reflect market conditions accurately, such a formula has to take into account the effect of shortages of skilled players, risks of injury or departure from the sport, or of loss of form and the objectives of the clubs. It is also likely that the marginal productivity of a player would vary between clubs. One club may require a particular type of player to make the best use of existing players and be prepared to pay very much more

[1] Players with more than four years' service ('veterans') can choose to have the clause excluded from their contracts, after which they automatically become free agents eligible to negotiate with any other club.

[2] Department of Education and Science, *Report of the Committee on Football* (Chairman: D. N. Chester), HMSO, London, 1968.

[3] Report No. 87, *op. cit.*

for him than would other clubs. On the supply side, transfer fees will be influenced by the willingness of clubs to sell star players, depending on whether a club has a large enough pool to cover the loss of a player, as well as on factors such as the satisfaction or otherwise of players with their current terms of employment.

The suggested compensation factors, which would considerably reduce transfer payments, may be more consistent with efforts to maximise profits than playing success.[1] A further weakness of the proposed formula was that it made no attempt to discount future returns, nor allowed for the possibility that current salary might not fully reflect potential in developing players. Doubts concerning the inflexibility of the system eventually led to the rejection of the formula by the league clubs in April 1978, and the substitution of freedom of contract subject to a negotiated transfer fee. In the event of a failure to agree under this system, now implemented, the figure is to be determined by an independent tribunal.

New UEFA rules for soccer player transfers in the EEC
The Union of European Football Associations (UEFA) has issued new regulations and guidelines to cover the movement of players between clubs in member countries of the European Economic Community after October 1978. Players are free to move to any club in the EEC on the expiry of their contract but, as in England, the two clubs must agree upon a transfer fee.[2] If there is no agreement on the size of the fee within 30

[1] Indeed, the maximisation of playing success may explain the present high transfer fees relatively to club revenues. It may, however, be easier to explain the higher transfer fees for outstanding players than for average players in terms of profit maximisation. Following the transfer of Trevor Francis to Nottingham Forest for £1 million, according to press reports, the club earned £1 million in nine months from success in the League Cup and European Cup and has already been offered a higher fee for Francis by an American club. High transfer fees may also be offset to some extent by the sale of other (not so highly skilled) players. Thus, the argument is that the general level of transfer fees is such that it can impose too heavy a burden on the less successful clubs, not that particular high transfer fees have no economic rationale.

[2] The multiplying factors in Table III suggest that fees would be fixed at a much lower figure than currently applies. Transfers within the period of a contract are not, however, subject to any restrictive regulations other than the agreement of both clubs. During the 1979-80 season an English international, Tony Woodcock, was transferred from Nottingham Forest to a West German club, FC Cologne, for a fee of £600,000—much lower than for comparable players transferred between English clubs. His contract would have expired at the end of the season when the formula would have provided an even lower fee.

[57]

TABLE III

THE NEW UEFA FORMULA FOR DETERMINING TRANSFER FEES FOR PROFESSIONAL SOCCER PLAYERS IN THE EUROPEAN ECONOMIC COMMUNITY

The Board of Experts shall apply as a rule the following principles:

- the amount of the indemnity (transfer fee) shall correspond to the gross income of the player (income earned through his activity as a footballer during the preceding season), multiplied by a coefficient factor which varies according to his age.

The gross income includes:

- the player's fixed wages
- the bonuses paid by the club
- the bonuses paid by the national association for international games, etc.
- the royalties received by the club for advertising on the jersey of the player.

The multiplying factors are as shown below.

Age	Multiplying factor
18 to 21 years	12
22 – 24 ,,	10
25 – 27 ,,	8
28 – 30 ,,	6
31 ,,	3
32 ,,	2
33 ,,	1

(These multiplying factors represent maximum indemnities, which must not exceed 2 million Swiss francs.)

---

days the matter is to be settled by a Board of Experts on the principles illustrated in Table III. The UEFA document also states it is desirable that the transfer system in each member country should be adapted as soon as possible to the joint system of the EEC countries.

As in North America, it is too soon to judge the long-run effects of increased freedom of contract.

(b) Product market competition—the challenge of Packer

Product market competition in international cricket is eased because traditionally a series of Test matches takes place between two teams. To introduce a new league would require the organisation of several teams with much higher development costs. Competing leagues have emerged, historically, in North American team sports despite such difficulties.[1]

After the North American experience there should be no surprise that the eventual outcome of WSC entry into international cricket was a compromise solution in which monopoly was restored to the product market. Yet the market may not be quite the same as before, since there will be more awareness of the threat of potential competition if the monopoly becomes too restrictive or fails to meet the changing tastes of consumers.

TV rights the initial cause of Packer's entry

The initial impetus for Kerry Packer's entry into international cricket was his failure to obtain from the Australian Cricket Board exclusive rights to televise the established Test series, and this led to the idea of organising the best players in the world into teams under his own control for the same purpose. This is an example of 'backward integration', such as may be undertaken by a retailer because his product is denied to him by a monopolist. That the WSC was able to engage 34 of the world's leading cricketers within a few months early in 1977 (and eventually over 50) indicates the low salaries offered by cricket at that time relative to other professional sports.

In England there are about 230 professional cricketers

---

[1] In 1890, following a dispute, baseball players formed their own league in competition with the established National League. But the so-called Players League suffered heavy financial losses and eventually collapsed. The National League was again challenged by the American Association in the 1890s when both leagues began to poach players from each other. But in 1903 the monopoly was restored with a National Commission over-seeing the two leagues. In 1913 the Federal League began organising and competing for players with the National League. This development eventually led to the baseball exemption from the anti-trust laws in 1922 (p. 54). During the inter-league war of this period total attendances fell substantially, possibly because of a decline in the quality of play as the increased number of teams employed minor league players. During the product market 'war' both total employment and wages of star players rose significantly.

This story has been repeated in other sports. The new football and basketball leagues of the 1960s were unable to overcome the competition of established teams in particular cities—the American Football League eventually merged with the National Football League. Success for a new league may, therefore, require member clubs to be located in cities not already represented by major league clubs. Even then there is an incentive for merger because of competition for players. Such an outcome would restore the effectiveness both of the player draft system, since the two leagues can arrange for their weakest teams to draft the better players sequentially, and of the contractual arrangements for players of member clubs in each league.

playing for first-class county clubs and engaged for some five months of the year. Henry Blofeld[1] suggests that in the summer of 1977 senior capped English players earned £3,500 and junior capped players £2,500, though these earnings were supplemented by appearance money and winning bonuses. Although established players may obtain £25,000 or more in their benefit years, after 10 or 15 years of low salaries, this sum does not compare with the salaries of up to £25,000 offered by WSC for up to 65 match days.

It is perhaps more difficult to explain the absence of entrepreneurial activity long before the appearance of Packer himself. Cricketers, like the authorities, appear to have accepted the inevitability of low incomes, not perceiving the potential for expanding the market.

Challenge and response

In response to the Packer challenge, the International Cricket Conference met in July 1977 and banned the 51 WSC players from Test cricket (and any other player who signed for WSC). It also recommended that each member country should take similar action in its domestic cricket competitions. In August the organisers of WSC cricket and representatives of their contracted players brought proceedings before the English High Court to contest the ICC and TCCB bans.

The court hearing extended over 31 days and involved the cricket authorities in legal costs of £250,000. The arguments put by the parties highlight the differences of view between the established authorities and the competing league.[2] The authorities' representatives argued that the structure and finances of cricket in the counties represented were dependent on Test match income, now under threat, which supported not only the first-class clubs but also cricket at lower levels. A further defence was that it cost a county club on average £30,000 over five years to convert a young player into an established county cricketer; in effect, WSC was poaching specifically trained labour and was able to pay significantly higher salaries only because it had not incurred the costs of training. Several players and the Secretary of the Cricketers' Association (CA) also appeared on behalf of the authorities. The CA Secretary

[1] *The Packer Affair*, Collins, London, 1978.

[2] *Greig and Others v. Insole and Others; World Series Cricket Pty Ltd. v. Same.*

argued that the WSC cricketers would use county cricket merely to retain their form and fitness, thus devaluing the competition.[1] WSC argued that the changes in the rules of the ICC and the consequent ban on WSC players were *ultra vires* and void as an unreasonable restraint of trade.

In summarising the case for WSC, Mr Justice Slade acknowledged five positive beneficial effects emerging from its promotion:

(i) it had offered much higher payments for star cricketers as well as secure and regular employment for three English winter seasons at a time of year when most of the players would otherwise have no guarantee of regular employment in the game;

(ii) it had stimulated new sponsors for traditional cricket;

(iii) It had brought out of retirement in Australia several talented players;

(iv) the promoters had initiated a coaching scheme for young players in New South Wales;

(v) it had increased public interest in the game.

Mr Justice Slade found for WSC on all points. He concluded it was straining the concept of loyalty too far for the ICC and TCCB to expect professional cricketers to enter into a self-denying ordinance not to play for a private promoter during the winter months, merely because such matters could detract from the profits of the ICC and TCCB.

Ultimately, the success or otherwise of WSC depended on whether or not exclusive rights to TV coverage of Test matches in Australia were obtained and whether an accommodation was made with the traditional cricket authorities. Agreement was reached on both matters in May 1979 (below). The accommodation would be significant if the established authorities were able in the long run to restrict the supply of star players to WSC by offering higher salaries. This response would require either short-term losses or improved product promotion, thus forcing WSC to recruit and train promising

[1] The Cricketers' Association (which is the players' 'union') maintained a consistently antagonistic stance against WSC players. Resolutions were put before a meeting in April 1979 providing that members should refuse to play with or against a county club signing *additional* WSC players or a county signing WSC players released by another county.

young players. In the early days of WSC, attendances were sparse; Wilson and Allan[1] estimated a loss of £1·2 million in 1977-78 and £890,000 in 1978-79, though much of the losses could be written off against the cost of buying more expensive alternative TV programmes.

WSC revenue and expenditure contrasted markedly with that of traditional cricket. In 1977-78 nearly half the total revenue was obtained from advertising, whilst, in addition to substantial expenditure on players' salaries, ground preparation and ground rental entailed considerable costs. There were signs of increasing interest in WSC matches and attendances were on a rising trend. Floodlit night games, in particular, proved to be popular. In the long run, new competition may have the effect of shifting the demand curve for international cricket to the right—raising the demand for cricket as a whole and increasing gate revenue at current prices for all games.

Continuing impact of Packer's marketing expertise

In May 1979 the Australian Cricket Board (ACB) granted PBL Sports Pty. Ltd. (a Packer company) the exclusive rights for 10 years to promote the programme of cricket organised by the Board and to arrange its televising and marketing (including sponsorship, advertising and players' endorsement of equipment). In addition, Packer's Channel Nine TV network was given exclusive rights to televise Australian Test and Sheffield Shield cricket for three years. It was agreed that the separate WSC programme would be abandoned, although many of its (by then) 68 players were on contracts of two years or more, with an unavoidable salary bill of up to £2 million. In return the ACB agreed to 'consider favourably' many of Packer's innovations including the introduction of 30-yard circles and restrictive field placings in limited-over matches, floodlit cricket and coloured clothing. The World Series logo would continue to be worn by Australians in one-day internationals.

Thus it appears that the Packer innovations and marketing skills are likely to have a permanent effect on international cricket. Even the Chairman of the ACB was forced to admit that

'the winner has been the game of cricket . . . the ACB has learned

[1] *Op. cit.*

[62]

a lot from the activities of World Series Cricket over the past two years. We have come to terms with the commercialism.'[1]

During the winter of 1979-80 a new type of triangular Test series took place in Australia between England, Australia and the West Indies, and the tour also included a number of one-day matches between the three sides (some under floodlights) enploying Packer innovations and marketing. The *rapprochement* between the cricket establishment and Packer has not been easy, however, and disputes have arisen over the size of guarantee offered to the tourists and over players' fees.

Summary

To sum up: The players have gained higher Test match fees and basic wages. A new wage agreement between the professional Cricketers' Association (CA) and the English counties provided for a minimum wage of £4,000 per annum plus a possible addition of £500 in bonuses and extra payments for County and Test caps. The CA's objective was to obtain a minimum wage of £5,000 by 1980. It is doubtful whether this would have been agreed without Packer and, indeed, it is unlikely that these higher payments can be sustained without new promotional activities.

The benefits to spectators will come in the form of more entertaining cricket. There will probably also be more respect for spectators. A failure to take account of consumer (spectator) preferences was illustrated by an incident in the 1979 season. In a Benson and Hedges Cup match the Somerset captain declared at the end of the first over of the day after only one run had been scored, thus losing to Worcestershire but ensuring that Somerset went through to the quarter-finals on the basis of a higher rate of taking wickets. But the spectators' admission fees were returned and, even though the captain's action was within the rules, the TCCB expelled Somerset from the competition at a cost to the county of between £2,500 and a possible £10,000 in prize money.

---

[1] Reported in the *Guardian,* 31 May 1979.

[63]

V. IS A COMPETITIVE MARKET VIABLE IN PROFESSIONAL TEAM SPORTS?

(i) *The market for players*

Historically, professional team sports have operated as *monopsonists* vis-à-vis* players in the factor market and monopolists *vis-à-vis* spectators in the product market. What are the effects of increased competition in the two markets?

The impact on uncertainty of outcome of the introduction of a free market in labour will clearly be influenced by the environment in the product market, including factors such as spectator potentials of the member clubs, revenue-sharing arrangements, and motivation of club owners. The ubiquity of market imperfection means that the case for a competitive market in which there are no restrictions on player mobility must rest mainly on theoretical rather than on empirical evidence. D. S. Davenport[1] described the situation in 19th-century baseball before the introduction of the reserve clause:

> 'The result in the early days of professional baseball was ravaging competition for players and a farce on the field. In 1869, the Cincinnati Red Stockings won 57 games without a loss. Salaries were so high and public interest so low that "no clubs could report any profits". The practice of "revolving", whereby a player could continually switch to a club that would pay him more, was the main cause. The baseball industry was suffering so badly that the clubs were forced to get together. The result in 1880 was the reserve clause or rule.'

Subsequently, uncertainty of outcome increased substantially, a majority of clubs showed a profit, and players' salaries doubled. The historical evidence also shows that, in searching for playing success, managements have persistently been able to find loopholes in the laws of the game. A continuing requirement for new rules emphasises, therefore, the problem of cartel cheating (II (*e*), p. 40).

Professor Rottenberg[2] has suggested that competitive mar-

---

[1] 'Collusive Competition in Major League Baseball: Its Theory and Institutional Development', *American Economist*, Fall 1969.

[2] 'The Baseball Player's Labour Market', *op. cit.*

kets, which are to be preferred on welfare grounds, would give as good aggregate results as alternative arrangements in sporting labour markets. This claim would seem to depend upon the predominance of the profit maximisation objective and other factors: the willingness and ability of club owners to sell off star players to other clubs as soon as their playing success becomes too pronounced and begins to erode their profits; negligible resistance by supporters to the sale of star players; the absence of league playing success as an entry qualification to other competitions; and a low degree of uncertainty about relative playing performance. The argument also ignores the possibility that it may take a substantial time to achieve a satisfactory degree of equality and that there may be permanent disruptive forces arising from variations in potential fan support for different teams.[1]

The hazards of thus re-allocating players would seem to be considerable, particularly since, insofar as profitability varies with playing success, it may not be possible for all clubs to be profitable at any given time, particularly when leagues are large. There is no obvious parallel to this relationship between structure and performance in the conventional competitive industry.

Yet it has been demonstrated that, even with a reserve clause, player drafts (as defined in III *(a)* (i), pp. 48-9) and profit-maximising owners, rules permitting the sale of player contracts among teams would lead to unequal playing strengths so long as clubs are located in market areas with very different revenue potentials.[2] Would then a free labour market lead to a markedly inferior outcome than one with restrictions on player mobility? Much would depend upon the rules in the product market (II *(e)*, p. 40). Player retention clauses may slow down the natural tendency for star players to gravitate towards the richer clubs, whilst reducing financial disparities between richer and poorer clubs through payment of transfer fees. This gravitation (but not a reduction in disparities) could equally well be achieved by long-term contracts of sufficient duration, say, five years or so, in view of the relatively short career of the average player.

[1] M. El Hodiri and J. Quirk, 'An Economic Model of a Professional Sports League', *Journal of Political Economy*, December 1971, demonstrate that the market areas in which teams are located must not differ from one another to such an extent that a team finds its gate receipts are more influenced by an increase in the playing strength of one club rather than another.

[2] El Hodiri and Quirk, *ibid*.

Further, the effect of retention rules is to re-distribute income from the player to a club, and this result may, by reducing the total costs of all clubs, make it possible for even the weaker to survive.[1]

Finally, restrictions on mobility may reduce the possibility that players are paid in accordance with their contribution to the revenue of the club rather than of the league as a whole. That is, a player's contribution towards increasing attendances at the games of his club (a private benefit) will result simultaneously in a reduction in attendance at games of other clubs in which the player does not participate (a social cost).[2] It is arguable, therefore, that a limited form of labour market restriction, voluntarily agreed by the clubs, is necessary for stability in the sporting product market, given that unequal revenue-sharing is regarded as impracticable. But even such a restriction may not be stable if there is competition in the product market.

(ii) *Are sports leagues natural monopolies?*

In inter-league competition (as with Packer), are sporting leagues natural monopolies in the sense that only one league in a given sport can be economically viable in the long run?[3] In part it would seem that the answer must be a function of the size of the market, the number of clubs divided into competing leagues, and their locations in relation to one another. In North America the entry of new leagues has always led to the destruction of the new league or its merger into the existing monopoly in the product market. Further, as W. C. Neale[4] points out, there is a natural tendency to compete on a wider basis.

'Where sporting competition is prevented by geographical difference the tendency is to enlarge the area . . . until . . . there is only one league. Thus we find that Australian, West Indian, Indian, Pakistani and English cricket, separated by about as much as is possible . . . merge into that great international cartel, the Test matches.

[1] Demmert, *op. cit.*

[2] Noll, *op. cit.*

[3] Individual clubs may also be regarded as natural monopolies where they are sited in cities capable of supporting only one club, though, again, this will be influenced by the revenue-sharing arrangements of the league organisation.

[4] 'The Peculiar Economics of Professional Sports', *Quarterly Journal of Economics*, Vol LXXVIII, No. 1, February 1964.

'Again, soccer . . . which is formally organised in teams merged in national leagues, has become a cartel of international matches. Since cartelisation is necessary not only to maximisation of profits but also, even especially, to maximisation of output, the geographical division of the market is an inherently unstable situation usually replaced by a naturally monopolistic firm whose market region is everywhere that the sport is played.'

Limited competition and inefficiency

In the United States separate leagues exist in various sports, but they are at least in part geographically separate, and they combine together each year to produce a World Series, as well as limiting economic competition between one another in various ways. Whether or not sporting leagues are natural monopolies, they engage in competition with other professional sports leagues (and to a lesser extent with other forms of entertainment), though this competition is often reduced by arranging the seasons to minimise fixture clashes—as in cricket and soccer until comparatively recently. We would expect a profit-maximising monopolist to raise price and restrict output relatively to a competitive market and/or to adopt relatively inefficient practices and be slow to change. High profits will, of course, under normal circumstances attract competitors. To forestall this effect, the league cartel may be prepared to admit new teams from time to time. Thus the various North American sports have had periods of expansion when new clubs were allowed to enter the leagues, although they are still small by European standards.

New entrants have generally been required to pay a franchise fee and to purchase a number of players from each member club, to the financial benefit of the existing cartel members. In Europe, periods of expansion are less common, perhaps because the objectives of the participants are to maximise utility rather than profit, and the size of the leagues is often relatively large from the outset. Here the problem may be not so much high prices and low output as general inefficiency and a failure to adapt to change, as the Packer episode suggests is true of cricket. Thus, even if merger is inevitable in the long run, the entry of competing leagues may provide advantages in inducing change which leads to a higher standard of performance and responsiveness to consumer preferences, to the benefit of both consumers and players.

VI. CONCLUSIONS

The product and labour markets of professional team sports are riddled with anti-competitive practices which in conventional industries would sometimes infringe monopoly and restrictive practices legislation and be opposed by economists on welfare grounds. Yet a number of features of such sports would seem to set them apart from other industries.

Joint product

1. Clubs are required to remain separate entities but to combine together in order to produce their joint output which, together with the dependence of the quality of output equally on the performance of each team, makes the market inherently unstable as long as some clubs are more able to raise revenues than others. This instability is likely to be stronger where sports organisers are motivated by the desire to maximise the playing success of their club rather than its profitability, which appears to be true in Britain and other countries, if not in North America.

Winners and losers in a cartel to produce uncertainty of results

2. Given that revenue is in part determined by playing success and that it is impossible for all clubs within a league to be successful in that sense, at any one time a virtuous circle may operate to maintain the playing success of the wealthy clubs, whilst the remainder of clubs are caught in a vicious circle of poverty and lack of success on the field of play. The larger the size of league in any given geographical area and the wider the dispersion of population in the locations of the member clubs, the stronger the probability that some clubs will make financial losses. The league organisation then operates as a cartel to re-distribute income and playing resources among the member clubs in order to ensure, as far as possible, uncertainty of outcome. Economists are generally opposed to such forms of cross-subsidisation on the ground that they lead to a misallocation of resources, but this argument does not carry over to the

sports industry because of the mutual inter-dependence of the clubs (firms).

3. Professional sports leagues may not always have adopted optimal price/output policies. It may not therefore be efficient to impose uniform admission prices on all member clubs. The tendency to fix low prices for major games results in a black market in tickets. A system of allowing consumers to tender for tickets according to ability and willingness to pay could overcome this problem.

4. It is questionable whether the major professional team sports in Britain can continue to operate with the present number of clubs at the top. In any event, team sports organisers would not seem to have exploited the market potential to the full: it requires identification of the potential for attracting additional spectators and sponsors, maximising TV and other media income, and presenting the product to attract various categories of spectator.

5. The established organisers of professional team sports appear to have given inadequate attention to revenue-sharing arrangements as a means of ensuring sporting equality. A more equal division of gate receipts may offset some of the problems arising from the weakening of labour market controls. The adoption of inefficient practices may reflect not only lack of competition but also lack of well-established property rights in the ownership of sports clubs.

6. Government has traditionally taken an active rôle in sports, perhaps because of external benefits. More recently, intervention has resulted from the external costs of crowd violence within and near sports grounds (though mainly limited to soccer) and from problems of safety in sports grounds, which have led to new legislation.

7. Unlike in the USA, monopolies and restrictive practices legislation has not been an issue. In the USA the exemption of baseball and other sports from the anti-trust laws has caused a fierce debate, but there seem to be grounds for treating professional team sports differently from other industries, even if the precise form of exception from customary restraints on behaviour is not yet clear.

New competition

8. In recent years professional team sports have had to face new challenges. Player unions have gained in strength, encouraged their members to seek redress in the courts for limitations on their freedom of employment, and negotiated collective agreements which effectively weaken the monopsonistic control of the employers over the labour market for players.

9. In response to the apparent lack of marketing expertise displayed by the established authorities and the attraction of large potential profits, entrepreneurs have begun to challenge the sporting establishment by attracting away star players and mounting their own tournaments. This development was seen first in international tennis, then in a professional soccer league in the USA, and most recently in the Packer entry into the international cricket market. Each of these challenges has raised the salaries of the star players, reducing the monopoly rents of the established authorities (or pushing them further into debt), and expanding total income by improved marketing of the product.

Freedom of contract

10. Freedom of contract for the players will make it more difficult to maintain uncertainty of outcome, although alternative policies may be introduced to offset this effect. In soccer, some of the suggested revisions imply transfer fees fixed at a lower sum than they would have reached under the old system. The rules may then be flouted. In extreme cases, freedom of movement for the players may result in a reduction in the size of league as competitive bidding raises salaries so high that some clubs can no longer compete. Unregulated competition in the product market may reduce the incomes of established clubs with the same result.

11. It is possible that lack of competition has led to various forms of inefficiency in the established leagues which increased competition will eliminate. In cricket, the established game may have to be made more attractive to the spectator if it is to survive in anything like its present form. WSC has shown the advantages of product innovation such as night cricket, other forms of entertainment at the ground, and changes of rules to make the game more exciting. Likewise, the North American

Soccer League has packaged the game in the professional manner adopted by the other major North American team sports.

12. Competition in professional team sports cannot be 'perfect' because of the spatial separation of clubs. But the notion of 'workable competition' is germane when public policy cannot easily produce reforms that would result in social gains that outweigh social losses for consumers.[1] The degree of concentration in an industry is here less important than innovation and entrepreneurship. Although sporting authorities are sole suppliers, it is always possible for new entrants, such as Packer, to remedy inefficient markets in such a way that the system responds, although slowly, to changes in competitive pressures. That soccer has not faced new entrants within established markets may reflect not only barriers to entry but also its spontaneous adaptation to new commercial challenges to a higher degree than cricket. Given potential entry, prohibition in general of non-competitive practices in professional team sports may yield small social gains but cause some social losses.

[1] Jesse Markham, 'An Alternative Approach to Workable Competition', *American Economic Review,* Vol. XI, 1950.

QUESTIONS FOR DISCUSSION

1. What distinguishes professional team sports from other types of sport and from conventional industry?

2. What factors determine the demand for professional sport? Is sports spectating an inferior good?

3. What role does uncertainty of outcome play in professional team sports? Can it justify restriction of competition in pricing and output decisions and in property rights in players?

4. Does the existence of black market prices for Cup Final tickets mean that the Football Association is a non-profit maximiser?

5. Is the market for professional sports inherently unstable? If so, in what ways is this true and is cross-subsidisation justifiable?

6. Explain why transfer fees for professional footballers have risen to sums sometimes in excess of £1 million. Do clubs pay large fees rather than develop their own players?

7. 'Cricket is more commercially backward than soccer'. Discuss this statement.

8. What would be the effects of the introduction of a totally free labour market in professional team sports?

9. Are there economic reasons why league authorities should regulate commercial sponsorship of individual member clubs?

10. Should the sports industry be exempted from monopoly and restrictive practices legislation?

FURTHER READING

Blofeld, H., *The Packer Affair*, Collins, London, 1978.

Commission on Industrial Relations, *Professional Football*, Report No. 87, HMSO, 1974.

Dabscheck, B., 'The Wage Determination Process for Sportsmen', *Economic Record*, March 1975.

——, 'Sporting Equality: Labour Market *vs.* Product Market Control', *Journal of Industrial Relations*, June 1975.

Demmert, H. G., *The Economics of Professional Team Sports*, Lexington Books, D. C. Heath and Co., Lexington, Mass., 1973.

Department of Education and Science, *Report of the Committee on Football* (Chairman: D. N. Chester), HMSO, 1968.

Hart, R. A., Hutton, J., and Sharot, T., 'A Statistical Analysis of Association Football Attendances', *Journal of the Royal Statistical Society*, Series C, Vol. 24, No. 1, 1975.

Hunt, J. W., and Lewis, K. A., 'Dominance, Recontracting and the Reserve Clause: Major League Baseball', *American Economic Review*, Vol. 6, No. 5, 1976.

El Hodiri, M., and Quirk, J., 'An Economic Model of a Professional Sports League', *Journal of Political Economy*, December 1971.

Jones, J. C. H., 'The Economics of the National Hockey League', *Canadian Journal of Economics*, February 1969.

Noll, R. G. (ed.), *Government and the Sports Business*, Studies in the Regulation of Economic Activity, The Brookings Institution, Washington DC, 1974.

Neale, W. C., 'The Peculiar Economics of Professional Sports', *Quarterly Journal of Economics*, Vol. LXXVIII, No. 1, February 1964.

Rivett, P., 'The Structure of League Football', *Operational Research Quarterly*, Vol. 26, No. 4, 1975.

Rottenberg, S., 'The Baseball Players' Labour Market', *Journal of Political Economy*, Vol. 64, June 1956.

Scully, G. W., 'Pay and Performance in Major League Baseball', *American Economic Review*, Vol. 64, December 1974.

Sloane, P. J., 'The Labour Market in Professional Football', *British Journal of Industrial Relations*, Vol. 7, July 1969.

——, 'The Economics of Professional Football: The Football Club as a Utility Maximiser', *Scottish Journal of Political Economy,* Vol. 18, June 1971.

——, 'Sporting Equality . . . A Comment', *Journal of Industrial Relations*, March 1976.

——, 'Restriction of Competition in Professional Team Sports', *Bulletin of Economic Research*, Vol. 28, No. 1, May 1976.

Some Recent IEA Publications

Occasional Paper 56

Whatever Happened to Productivity?
Tenth Wincott Memorial Lecture
GRAHAM HUTTON

1980   36pp+8pp Statistical Supplement   £1·00

'A searing attack on Britain's "catastrophic performance" in the international productivity stakes.

Mr Hutton blames unions, Luddism, the growth of the state and spineless management for Britain's performance, which have resulted in our declining from second place in 1953 to twentieth in the list of the 24 leading industrial nations.'

The Times

Hobart Paper 84

Protectionism Again . . .?
Causes and Consequences of a Retreat from Freer Trade to Economic Nationalism
DAVID GREENAWAY and CHRISTOPHER MILNER

1979   88pp   £1·50

'The increasingly vocal arguments for protection of British industry are strongly criticised in a study published today . . . The authors examine tariffs as a way to correct market failures, paying particular attention to the infant industry argument.'

Financial Times

Readings 23

The Prime Mover of Progress
A Symposium on
The Entrepreneur in Capitalism and Socialism
ISRAEL KIRZNER, LESLIE HANNAH, NEIL MCKENDRICK, NIGEL VINSON, KEITH WICKENDEN, SIR ARTHUR KNIGHT, SIR FRANK MCFADZEAN, P. D. HENDERSON, D. G. MACRAE, IVOR PEARCE

1980   xiv+154pp   £3·50

Papers on 'The Role of the Entrepreneur':

The essence: 'alertness'—The entrepreneur in history—Three 'cameos' of entrepreneurs—Public and private sectors compared and contrasted—Villain to hero?—Public policy

[75]

Hobart Paperback 13
Over-ruled on Welfare
A 15-year investigation into private preferences and public policy based on surveys in 1963, 1965, 1970, 1978 into priced choice between state and private services
RALPH HARRIS and ARTHUR SELDON

1979 xxx+249pp With 6 Appendices, 10 Charts and 43 Tables
£3·00

'. . . the ideas adumbrated so readably in this book do have most plausible application . . . the IEA's splendidly anti-bureaucratic principles are an invaluable antidote to public sector Toryism as much as socialism.' .

The Economist

Readings 21
The Taming of Government
STEPHEN C. LITTLECHILD, GORDON TULLOCK,
A. P. L. MINFORD, ARTHUR SELDON, ALAN BUDD,
CHARLES K. ROWLEY
With an Introduction by LORD ROBBINS

1979 xxiii+136pp £3·00

'If Mr Heseltine really wants to phase out the functionaries he should take some tips from . . . *The Taming of Government.* Instead of running a Ministry bank to finance retired mandarins' stately descent into the marketplace, he would bring competition into the sacred precinct of Whitehall itself.'

Leader, *Daily Mail*

Occasional Paper 55
Choice in European Monetary Union
Ninth Wincott Memorial Lecture
ROLAND VAUBEL

1979 32pp 80p

'The lecture deserves a wider audience, not just because Dr Vaubel pours a douche of cold water on all the present efforts towards European Monetary Union, but because he advances a practical way in which European Monetary Union might be reached through an idea very much on the lines of Professor Hayek's thinking: allowing a "good" new European currency to drive out the "bad" national ones.'

Hamish McRae, *Guardian*